Closed Ranks

An Experiment in
Mental Health Education

Closed Ranks ~

An Experiment in Mental Health Education

Elaine Cumming & John Cumming

SOCIOLOGIST   PSYCHIATRIST

Published for The Commonwealth Fund
by Harvard University Press
Cambridge, Massachusetts · 1957

To
Our Sons
Ian and David

Acknowledgments

Although this book was originally presented as a doctoral dissertation in Radcliffe College of Harvard University, it has been completely rewritten for lay readers.

Invaluable help and encouragement were given us during the preparation of the original manuscript by Professor Frederick C. Mosteller of Harvard University, who spent many hours on the material and manuscript. Dr. Kaspar D. Naegele, now of the University of British Columbia, worked so closely with us in developing the major theoretical interpretations of our field experience that we feel that we owe to him our greatest intellectual debt.

The influence of Talcott Parsons is strong in our work; all of our general concepts are rooted in his general theory of action. Nevertheless, the specific conceptual structure developed here is our own, and we take full responsibility for it.

We are indebted to the National Opinion Research Center, and to Dr. Shirley A. Star in particular, not only for permission to use their interview schedule but for the exchange of ideas which took place between us. At this point the concepts and formulations which underlay the NORC interview schedule and which were more explicitly expressed in NORC's codes, classifications, and preliminary summaries of the interview materials, are such an integral part of our thinking about our interview results that it is impossible now to tell precisely what in this area is essentially theirs and what is essentially our own. We hope that this exchange, which is so valuable a part of any research undertaking, has proved also to be beneficial to NORC.

We wish to thank the team of men and women who helped us plan and carry out our educational program, especially Neil Agnew, Stanley Rands, and David Smith. We are particularly grateful to Dr. Morgan Martin for his gifts of time and talent.

We can never really thank the people who resolutely did what turned out to be a very difficult piece of field work. They are Mary Morrison, Lori MacKay, Betty Hauser, Sidney Parsons, William Carment, Mary Agnew, Vincent Mehmel, and Geoffrey Glover.

The field study described herein was supported by the Commonwealth Fund, New York, through a generous grant to the Psychiatric Services Branch of the Department of Health of the Province in which we worked. Dr. D. G. Mc-Kerracher, Director of this Service, and all of his staff gave support and encouragement throughout the field work.

ELAINE CUMMING
JOHN CUMMING

1957

Foreword

In the past decade, mental health has come to be recognized as a part of public health. This recognition has added impetus to efforts to go beyond the treatment of mental illness and to look toward the possible prevention of such illness and toward minimizing the consequences of mental illness. The public health approach entails the application of scientific knowledge to community efforts to deal with the mass aspects of disease. How can the health practices and conditions of a population be influenced so as to minimize the development or spread of any disease? How can persons who have been handicapped by disease be restored to a greater measure of functional effectiveness? Approaches may vary for any given disease and population, but by and large they require that the population be reached, that beliefs, practices, and environmental conditions be modified in keeping with scientific knowledge on etiology, therapy, and rehabilitation.

Health education has an impressive record in the field of physical health. Large segments of our population have been thoroughly persuaded that the maintenance of health is a goal to be actively pursued. Except among relatively deprived groups, there is a widespread acceptance of such measures as regular medical and dental check-ups, balanced diets, and immunization against diseases which tend to have serious sequelae. In general, threats to health are to be systematically avoided whenever possible. Indeed, concern about sanitation, healthful living conditions, and diet has had its fad-like aspects in America. But many diseases which were feared inordinately and which carried a social stigma have either been brought under control or been rendered subject to effective action rather than to ostracism. By and large, efforts are made to deal with illness in such a way as to protect society and to restore the patient to health.

Health education in the field of mental illness has a formidable task. No facile formulae for the recognition of mental illness can be offered. There are no simple directives whose implementation will serve to ward off or prevent mental illness. The goals of mental health education have been rather to produce understanding—understanding of self and others, understanding of the various antecedents and manifestations of mental illness, understanding of the process whereby a biological organism becomes a human personality with its sensitivities and vulnerabilities. There are, of course, vast gaps in our knowledge of these phenomena. Furthermore, understanding of human behavior, that most common and seemingly simple subject of human discussion, cannot readily be conveyed through slogans or simple descriptive statements. For these reasons, mental health educational programs have had to be tentative, even groping.

The experiment in mental health education which Elaine and John Cumming here report represented a concentrated effort to change attitudes toward mental illness and the mentally ill in a single community. Their goal was both concrete and practical. They had observed the coldness of many communities to patients returning from mental hospitals: patients, released as recovered or markedly improved, are often unwelcome, feared, isolated. Changing such attitudes would favor the more complete rehabilitation of former patients.

The Cummings were aware that ignorance and fear of mental illness are widespread. They wisely desisted from a frontal attack on these attitudes. They point out that ignorance and fear are not merely the result of the lack of information about mental illness, but are derived from and maintained by personal and community needs. At the start of their project, however, it seems fair to say that the Cummings were not aware of the intensity of the feelings and functions underlying public attitudes toward mental illness. It is significant that the nature of public attitudes toward mental illness had hardly been explored at the time they undertook this enterprise. Indeed, the present volume constitutes a major contribution to our knowledge of public response to mental illness.

Social life is pleasant and indeed possible only when our interactions with others achieve a high measure of predictability coupled with the feeling that we understand what is going on and that others understand us. Mental illness threatens this predictability and understanding. It manifests itself in interpersonal difficulties and it tends to disrupt our most intimate and significant relationships. In this respect it is markedly different from physical illness. Physical illness may entail both pain and suffering for the patient and anguish for those closest to him. Prolonged chronic illness may even cause severe tensions within the family or in other intimate relationships, but by and large compassion far outweighs other sentiments. One identifies with the patient, shares his feelings of unhappiness at the inconvenience and deprivations that result from his illness. If the illness is mild, or one where the prognosis is good even though discomfort is severe, the hospital room may be a place of jollity once the crisis is passed. Friends drop by to congratulate the patient on his progress toward recovery and to cheer up patient and family. Even if there are residual impairments, one rejoices with the patient that things turned out as well as they did.

With mental illness, the situation is vastly different. The patient is "not himself." One can feel sorry for him, but few of us can truly sympathize with the patient whose moods are inappropriate, whose actions violate the expectations others hold for him, and whose interpretations of others seem so distorted, so unpredictable. From early childhood, most of us begin to pick up stereotypes and epithets which set the mental patient off as a different breed. Yet the knowledge that anyone may be vulnerable to mental illness and that one is not always able to control his feelings or even his actions may make the thought of mental illness a disturbing threat.

The Cummings developed their program within a community whose citizens had achieved little awareness of their own attitudes toward mental health and mental illness. The educational team made contacts with appropriate leaders and officials within the local community; but they did not have the advantage of having been asked by local leaders to conduct the program which they felt was needed. Mental health educational activities tend most often to be centered around formal or official organizations such as mental hygiene societies, parent–teacher associations and similar groupings of interested citizens. Having no formal sponsor in this community, the Cummings attempted to work most closely with several voluntary groups whose program interests were relevant to mental health, though the groups themselves would not have used the term.

The techniques and the materials used by the Cummings are being used in other mental health programs every day. Any program entails a selection from among a wide variety of techniques and approaches. The most commonly heard injunction to the health educator or indeed to anyone who hopes to change attitudes or practices in a community is, "Start where the community is." But one must frequently feel his way for some time before knowing quite where the community stands. Shall one use movies and discussion groups in which members can express fully some of their own concerns? Sometimes this approach will achieve one's ends admirably. At other times more anxiety may be mobilized than can be handled within the context of a public meeting.

Any program, then, requires a selection among alternative approaches based on an assessment of local conditions. The local setting almost always poses some obstacles to ideal program design, necessitating compromises. Faced with the realities of any given situation, some experts will favor one alternative, others a different one. Retrospectively, it is always easy to say which alternatives or compromises were "wrong." A detailed account of any football game will give the "Monday morning quarterback" a chance to explain how he might have run a more effective offensive. The fact is that we can only hope to understand why some approaches worked and others didn't.

The need for program evaluation is widely recognized, but seldom met. There are several reasons for this. One is the simple matter of cost. It is often as costly to determine whether one has effected a change through one's efforts in an educational or therapeutic program as it is to provide the services that constitute the program. Related to cost is the fact that the adequate evaluation of any program aimed at changing beliefs and behaviors is among the most difficult of social science research tasks. Most educational or community service programs have multiple objectives, not all of which can be adequately evaluated. Moreover, persons strongly motivated to carry out a practical task of education or service often do not see the need for systematic evaluation. Indeed, the suggestion that it might be well to see whether a program is achieving the objectives set for it may be seen by some devoted workers as a threat to the very premises upon which they have built their life work. It was, then, a happy circumstance that the Cummings were interested both in trying to bring about a change in attitudes and in assessing whether they had in fact done so. Equally fortunate was the fact that the Commonwealth Fund recognized the value of carrying out such a study and provided the necessary funds.

There are many aspects to the question of program effectiveness. Any one study can deal with only a few of these. Is one reaching the population for whom the program was designed? Is the message understood and can it be verbalized or, even better, put into action by those for whom it was intended? Beyond this, does the program make a difference? In reality, this "big question" becomes in itself many, many questions. *How* does it make a difference? To whom? Under what circumstances? The Cummings chose a relatively proximate goal: to ascertain whether the community educational program would diminish people's feelings of distance and estrangement from former mental patients and would increase their feelings of social responsibility for the problem of mental illness. They found that their program did not achieve these goals. The research team which attempted to ascertain the attitudes of Blackfoot citizens after the program encountered hostility and a great deal of apparent anxiety.

The Cummings have courageously attempted to find out why their initial goals were not achieved. In so doing they have produced what is perhaps the most thorough evaluation of a mental health educational program yet achieved. They specified their criteria of assessment. They devised measures of the variables with which they were concerned. They ascertained attitudes and beliefs of the local population prior to the program and at the conclusion of their educational efforts. They obtained comparable data for a "control" community. Herewith they are presenting the evidence in full, including their techniques of data collection, the data bearing on before-after comparisons, and the unexpected reactions of the community. In attempting to understand these unexpected reactions, the Cummings have formulated a basic hypothesis as to the nature of societal response to the topic of mental illness—a hypothesis difficult to prove conclusively, but one which other workers will want to bear in mind both in their community programs and in their research efforts.

As the Cummings themselves point out, there are certain difficulties inherent in linking an evaluation study with program personnel. When a team of workers attempts to assess its own effectiveness, there are some questions that they cannot themselves answer or even ask directly of their subjects. Were they seen by significant community leaders as outsiders with an axe to grind? Did they inadvertently offend local sensibilities? Were there warring local factions whose existence would not be revealed to anyone associated with the program? Such things can lead to the kind of rejection experienced by the team. One may wonder also at the extent to which so intensive a program in so small a community may have overwhelmed the local citizenry. Essentially all the adult members of the community were interviewed as to their attitudes. We do not know how widespread were the discussion of the interview or the rumors as to its meaning. The evaluation itself may have been seen as a threat to the privacy which surrounds certain types of beliefs, particularly in a population which does not habitually examine its beliefs.

The Cummings have made a cogent analysis of the problem of changing beliefs and attitudes toward mental illness. Because any single program is unique, one cannot yet say whether the reactions the Cummings experienced are inherent in the attempt to change views of mental illness. Quite possibly such reactions occur with high frequency but go undetected when the educational program is less intensive and its impact more diffused over a larger population. In any event, mental health educators will want to be forewarned and forearmed with the experience which is here recorded and the formulations and suggestions which Elaine and John Cumming have derived from their experience.

JOHN A. CLAUSEN

Contents

Part I

The Case: An Attempt to Modify Attitudes toward Mental Illness

Part II

The Empirical Analysis

Part III

The Theoretical Analysis

List of Tables

Nebuchadnezzar

One morning when they came to rouse me
From my imperial sleep they found me
Not as a proud emperor sleeping,
But as a hideous monster creeping.
One said: "What manner of thing is this?"
Another: "No denizen of palaces!"
And thereupon into the wilderness they sent
Me, without crown or raiment.

J. C. HALL in *The New Statesman and Nation* (October 17, 1953)

Introduction

This book is partly a narrative and partly an analysis. It is the story of a controlled experiment in mental health education which had surprising results, and a report of the analyses which followed over the ensuing two years.

The experiment was an attempt by a group of enthusiastic people to change a community's attitudes toward mental illness—from what we supposed were bad attitudes to what we defined as good ones. We embarked upon this attempt with high hopes, we planned carefully, we worked hard, and yet when the experiment was over it looked very much as if we had failed. This book is a report of what we did, what happened, how we came to decide that what had happened was more complex than a simple failure, and what we learned from our efforts and from our reflections about them.

The reader is asked to remember throughout this book that this work was done in 1951 and that in the ensuing years we, as well as he, have become wiser. However, despite the lapse of time, not many controlled field experiments in mental health education have been reported, and so we are presenting this material in the hope that it will be helpful to those working on the broad front of treatment and reha- bilitation of the mentally ill.

We attempted only one quite simple thing in our experi- ment—to modify attitudes toward the mentally ill with tech- niques and material then commonly in use—but our reflection upon the unexpected results of this attempt kept leading us back to our experience with the mentally ill, especially in mental hospitals. We have included, therefore, a good deal of general and specific information from such sources and have tried to synthesize these two aspects of our professional experience into a coherent whole.

Our frame of reference throughout is sociological; that is, we are primarily concerned not with the nature of mental illness, but with the role of the mentally ill in society. Our analysis is therefore only partial, and leaves a lot unsaid. However, it focuses on an aspect of mental illness—its social control—which is often neglected.

In the course of analyzing our experience we have often wanted to digress into a discussion of various approaches to mental health education and ways of evaluating them. Fortu- nately, since this experiment was done, Louisa P. Howe has published a definitive statement on this subject.[40a] We com- mend it to our reader as a frame of reference for the general problem of which we are attacking one particular facet.

Briefly, we believe we have made one crude stroke on a nearly empty canvas; we hope it may inspire others to add more so that eventually a coherent picture may emerge.

Part I

The Case: An Attempt to Modify Attitudes toward Mental Illness

The General Context
of the Study

1. *The Setting*

Our project was an attempt to understand and to change attitudes toward mental health and mental illness. Its special setting was the expanding Psychiatric Service Branch of the Department of Health in Prairie Province in Canada. This service had in the recent past rapidly increased treatment and prevention facilities, with an accompanying increase in staff of all kinds. Many discussions among those responsible for the "prevention" aspects of this service (especially as performed in out-patient clinics) had led us to the belief that very little is known about the nature of "preventive psychiatry" or about the nature of public attitudes, either good or bad, toward mental illness.

In spite of this lack of formal knowledge, the service has been engaged in an intensive and extensive training program for the medical residents, student nurses, and psychiatric nurses of the Province. The number involved in these programs at any one time is quite high, running to a staff of over 700 people, the majority of whom are psychiatric nurses. While this training scheme was building, it became evident that it had two aspects: the teaching of technical knowledge about mental illness, and the manipulation of attitudes toward the mentally ill. Those who planned and executed the programs began to suspect that the former was much easier to accomplish than the latter.

Coincidentally with the local expansion of the psychiatric services, a great interest had been aroused in "mental health education" among both the professional staff of the service and certain lay organizations such as the Canadian Mental Health Association. At the time of this study, the latter organization maintained its only paid Provincial secretary and full-time office staff in Prairie Province, although this local interest was parallel to a general increase in activity in the field at the national level. Many established methods of public education were being used, including pamphlets, study kits, talks, and films. The practicing psychiatrists and nurses, and especially the research workers, in the Service became interested in the efficacy of these methods, and questions arose: "What good is it all doing?" "Do these methods have any effect at all?"

In the meantime the local psychiatrists and social workers were fully aware that the attitudes toward the mentally ill which prevailed among the lay population were making it extremely difficult to rehabilitate the patients from large hospitals. Because there are close to 4,000 mental hospital beds in the Province—serving a population of approximately 800,000—it is of crucial importance at the practical level to know why it is so difficult to re-establish ex-patients in their communities. Not only have social workers told us that the reintegration of the patient with his family and community is the most difficult part of their job, but discussions with patients in mental hospitals and even in psychiatric wards of a general hospital have revealed that the patients themselves are acutely sensitive to the rejection which they feel awaits them upon their return home. We noticed that when the technique of role-playing was first employed in group therapy, the patients usually elected to role-play their return to the community, in an attempt to desensitize themselves to what they felt would be a traumatic experience.

In short, the service was faced simultaneously with two closely related problems: attitudes among the lay population which were crucial to discharge policy, and attitudes among their own staff which were crucial to good treatment.*

2. *The Orientation*

At the time of the study, the members of our research team were influenced in their thinking by reports of research into the nature of attitudes toward ethnic minorities. It has long been observed that people are not on the whole very accepting of minority group members and that this rejection has tended to be of a blind and uninformed sort, such as we felt characterized the rejection of the mentally ill. Attitudes toward minorities appear to be immovable except under certain very specific conditions.[22] Because we thought that we were dealing with similarly immovable ideas, we felt it unlikely that an educational program composed mostly of mass media would be particularly effective in achieving a change in the desired direction. For example, Williams has reported[94] that attempts to break down prejudice between ethnic groups have been extremely disappointing when the usual didactic methods have been used, and both Williams

---

* Since the time of this study we have had the opportunity of working intensively with nurses in a mental hospital. Much of our success in changing their attitudes toward their patients and their work resulted from the approach which we developed when we analyzed the experiment described in this volume. These very encouraging results are described in part in *Psychiatry*, Vol. 19, Nos. 1, 3, and 4, 1956, and in part in a volume soon to appear under the sponsorship of the National Institute of Mental Health, Bethesda, Md.

and Allport[4] have suggested that prejudiced attitudes are "functional" for some personalities, and Adorno et al.[3] have made the same point. We began by expecting that some people would change their attitudes more than others and that we could make a useful analysis of the difference in degree of change. However, we ended by discovering that our educational program had had almost no effect at all, and so we came to be interested in examining the function of these rejecting attitudes toward the mentally ill for society rather than for any particular types of personality. We finally reformulated the problem of the rejection of the mentally ill in terms of this failure of our "mental health education" program and included the two problems in an over-all analysis of attitudes toward mental health and mental illness.

3. The Plan

Our study was designed to investigate *to what extent and in what directions attitudes toward mental illness are changed by an intensive educational program.* Throughout this investigation, one of us (E. C.—sociologist) acted as planner and analyst, the other (J. C.—psychiatrist), as co-planner and education director. Although there was no overlap in the work of analysis and education, informal contact and program planning contact assured constant communication. Analysis, therefore, was not independent of the educational program in the strict sense.

In order to carry out our investigation, two communities, called here Blackfoot and Deerville, were chosen from an area of Prairie Province known to be reasonably homogeneous. The communities were found through examination of census data to be very similar in such characteristics as age, ethnicity, and occupation; our long-standing personal knowledge of the area was also taken into account. The community chosen for experimentation has approximately 1,500 people, and that chosen as a control approximately 1,100. These two towns are both on the cross-Canada railroad and are separated geographically by 150 miles.

To approach the problem of measuring attitudes toward mental illness, a questionnaire was developed containing two attitude scales of the Guttman type.[86] This was administered to the whole adult population of the experimental community and to 107 randomly selected adults in the control community just before a six-month intensive educational program—carried out in the experimental community only. (It has been suggested to us that this period of time was too short—and it must seem so to those accustomed to a slower-paced program of five or ten years. Six months is, however, considered too long by others—and indeed it must seem so to those who evaluate after one meeting. However, as Louisa P. Howe says in the work cited,[40a] one cannot do everything in one program—it is impossible to use more than one period of time. Six months was chosen on "common sense" grounds of practical experience.)

Immediately after the program the same measurement was repeated in both places so that we could see if the town in which the educational program had been carried out had changed more than that in which there had been no program.

In order to enrich our experiment by discovering in detail how people conceptualized the "mental illness" they responded to on the questionnaire, interviews* were held both

---

* The interview schedule used was developed by Dr. Shirley A. Star of the National Opinion Research Center, who will report a full account of the structure of public attitudes toward mental illness. We include a copy of the interview schedule along with data about our sample in Appendix I, but we shall not make any systematic analysis of our interview material. From time to time, where it is useful to the development of our story, we will call on certain selected results. For a full picture of public responses to this interview the reader is referred to Dr. Star's forthcoming volume, *The Dilemmas of Mental Illness.* Our own questionnaire used the term "mental illness" repeatedly, but we purposely did not specify what was meant by it. Thus people were forced to respond to it according to their own implicit definition of the phrase. The intensive interview allowed us to discover the range of implicit definitions in the population.

before and after the educational program. One hundred were conducted before and 70 after, both times with a random sample of the adults of our experimental community. We propose to discuss the technical details of the sample and the interviewing in Appendix I. The following chapter describes the experimental community and our experience in it.

The Community

1. *The Qualities Desired*

The community which we chose as the subject of our study we call Blackfoot; the control we call Deerville.

We felt the selection of these communities to be a very important step, because certain problems might be avoided through a careful choice. We wanted a town for our experiment small enough to permit a survey of all the adults and to provide a reasonable expectation that our educational program would be available to the whole population. On the other hand, we wanted it large enough to yield an analyzable group of people. It had to be close to our headquarters in the capital city of the Province in order to allow us to move easily back and forth during the winter no matter what the weather. We did not want a community of mixed ethnic origin because we were not able to speak foreign languages and we wished to avoid biases arising from incompletely acculturated people whose attitudes toward mental illness were substantially different from those of the English-speaking population. The community in which we worked should be settled and stable, with a nearly unchanging population, yet at the same time be representative of at least part of the Province.

2. *The People*

Blackfoot, the town of our final choice, lies in a long and fertile valley in the southeast corner of the Province. It had 1,313 citizens in 1926, and by 1951 this total had climbed to about 1,500. For Prairie Province this is a stable picture; population predictions made by the Provincial Government list Blackfoot as unlikely either to grow or to decline.

The population of Blackfoot contains a preponderance of older people and a dearth of children. In fact, about 10 per cent of the population is over seventy years of age, as compared with between 4 and 6 per cent for the country as a whole. There are a few more females than males in Blackfoot, and by far the largest group of people is married; there are a small number of widowed and a tiny group of divorced people.

The town has about 450 homes; most of them are modern, well-kept, single-family units. The number of rooms per dwelling is high and the number of people per room is low. Of the total number of dwelling units, more than half are owner-occupied and without a mortgage. This high percentage of mortgage-free homes is indicative of the stability of this community.

3. *The Style of Life*

The "style of life" in Blackfoot was very well known to us before we began our study—we had spent most of our lives close by. It is a wealthy town—three people are reputed millionaires—and it is, in a sense, a very proud and conservative town. That people take satisfaction in their individualism is illustrated by a story told by a long-time resident: when the members of the Library Board canvassed the town for donations with which they proposed to purchase a small building to house the local library, they could not raise the four hundred dollars necessary for the purchase. One wealthy citizen said to the canvasser, "If people want to read books, let them buy them."

To be just to the people of Blackfoot, however, their individualism should be put into its proper context, where it does not appear anti-intellectual as the example above suggests. Lipset,[49] studying the political aspects of Prairie Province, writes:

[Prairie Province] is a unique and rewarding place for a social scientist to do research, for the province contains a larger proportion of lay social scientists than any other area I have visited. The farmers are interested in their society and its relations to the rest of the world. Winter after winter, when the wheat crop is in, thousands of meetings are held throughout the province by political parties, churches, farmers' educational associations, and cooperatives. There are informal gatherings, also, in which farmers discuss economic and political problems. Not hedged in by the necessity of punching a time clock daily, these farmers who have come from every part of Europe and North America, have frequent sessions in which they consider the ideas of Adam Smith, Karl Marx, William Morris, Henry George, James Keir Hardie, William Jennings Bryan, Thorstein Veblen, and others. . . . Almost every English-speaking farmer subscribes to three or four farm weeklies, which are veritable storehouses of economic and political debate. . . .

Lipset's enthusiasm for the Blackfoot people—and they are essentially the ones he is describing, since the beginnings of the political movement he studied arose there—may seem a little excessive, but it is emphasized in order to remove them from the category of "hill-billies" or "hicks," in which they most certainly do not belong. Thus, when our respondent says, "Let them buy their own books," no doubt he tacitly adds, "as I have done."

As Lipset has said, these are a people who are used to meeting and considering new ideas—albeit cautiously. The discussion forum is part of their way of life. In Western Canada, moreover, new ideas have always come on foot—Blackfoot people had traditionally welcomed itinerant teachers and preachers. Mental health educators could fit very comfortably into this tradition.

The town has many attractive homes and well-kept lawns and gardens. In sharp contrast, the two school buildings are unattractive and old; one was built in 1875, early for this part of the world, and has never been properly renovated. Inside, both schools are dark and quite unpleasant, and yet a large number of public meetings take place there because there is no town hall or civic center. Just outside Blackfoot stands an agricultural experiment station operated by the Dominion Government. Its presence has added impetus to planting and caring for trees and gardens; in the local weekly paper the town is called "Blackfoot the Beautiful."

The experimental station is staffed by townsfolk with the exception of a small group of professional people who have come from larger centers, in many cases some years ago.

Blackfoot, like all small towns, has a very large number of organizations, social clubs, church groups, choirs, sports clubs, service clubs, and fraternal organizations. An agricultural representative of the Provincial Government reported that, while trying to interest these groups in building a community center, he had counted over seventy formal organizations! There is a high degree of overlap among their executives and memberships, and evidence from the weekly newspaper shows that attendance is usually poor. One editorial complained that of the 140 members of the Board of Trade, a relatively healthy organization, only 14 turned out to a meeting at which important policy decisions were to be made. Again, this pattern of maximum memberships and minimum attendance is probably common to many small towns.

When this phenomenon of overorganization is discussed with the local residents, they explain that the clubs are all dying, that now and then a new one is formed in the hope that it will be vital and alert and will "get things done," but in the end it is only one more weak and sickly organization added to the total number. Blackfoot people frequently complain about this situation in conversation, and they tend to blame civic ineffectualness upon the number of obligations people have to their various societies. The following casual comments recorded in the field are typical: "It's no use approaching some organizations because they don't do anything." "Oh, I keep out of the organizations; I only belong to five." There are, of course, a great number of people in the town who belong to no organization at all, while others belong to as many as twelve or fifteen. A local Mounted Policeman told us that it was absolutely essential for him to belong to five or six in order to be accepted in the community at all; it is very difficult to refuse membership in organizations in small towns. We received the impression that up to a point multiple membership in civic organizations is directly related to prestige in the community. Those with multiple memberships have high—but not the highest— prestige, and those without such memberships either lack prestige entirely or, on the other hand, enjoy the highest social position.

A search of the Provincial archives confirmed our informal impression that the town of Blackfoot was settled, like the surrounding country, in the last quarter of the nineteenth century, chiefly by English and Scottish immigrants who purchased very large tracts of land and for a time ran huge "country estates" patterned on English land-holding models. This type of land operation was not economical on the Canadian prairies and eventually these estates were broken up into manageable farms. Many of the families who pioneered the district still remain in Blackfoot, and it is to them that people refer when they say, "You can't get anywhere in this town unless you came in with the old pioneers." It is this group of old pioneers and their children and grandchildren who have the highest prestige and yet do not belong to formal organizations.

The community is about 95 per cent Anglo-Saxon in origin. The remaining 5 per cent are a small group of somewhat underprivileged Métis, a people descended from Indian women and French or Scottish fur traders. The Métis are not integrated into either Indian or white society. They live in a section of town called "Germantown" which, although no Germans have ever lived in it, received its name, a reflection of its undesirability, during the First World War. This little area stands in contrast to the well-kept homes of the rest of the community. It is a collection of light wooden shacks covered with black building paper, without water or plumbing, and constituting by contrast a slum in an otherwise prosperous and attractive town.

4. *The Choice*

Our experimental community, then, had the following advantages for the research: it was settled and stable, with a homogeneous population; it was fairly representative of the whole southeastern section of the Province; and it was easily accessible to us. Its "conservatism" we felt to be a virtue because useful changes in attitude, if they were effected there, might be even easier to produce in a more "progressive" community. Perhaps a quotation best illustrates this point: a colleague who had left Blackfoot many years before exclaimed upon hearing our purpose, "If you can change attitudes in Blackfoot, you should have no trouble changing them anywhere else in the world." We have stressed Black-foot's conservatism, but while it is probably less "progressive" than most of Prairie Province, the people, we have found, are more friendly and approachable than those of the older, longer-settled East.

All that we lacked was a suitable control community. This we needed because the activities of the Canadian Mental Health Association in the Province might in themselves be changing attitudes. To control our experiment, we chose Deerville, a community of similar composition and size, not so close to Blackfoot as to be affected by the educational program that was to take place there, but not so far away as to be outside the homogeneous southeast section of the Province. Deerville lacks an experimental station (although for many years it had a Provincial jail) and it lacks the small underprivileged group of Métis, but otherwise it is comparable to Blackfoot. Interviews with Deerville citizens yielded the familiar story of "overorganization" that we were to hear so often in our experimental community.

We planned to administer attitude measurement questionnaires in Deerville to a sample of about 100 adults both before and after the educational program in Blackfoot, but we did not plan to make any further exploration there. The purpose of the control community was to make sure that attitudes throughout the Province as a whole were not changing as rapidly as they might be in Blackfoot.

The Educational Program

1. *The Assumptions*

We designed the content and method of our educational program in a planning committee of two psychiatrists, two educationalists (one a professional mental health educator), and a sociologist. There is no tried and true way of presenting such a program; unfortunately, there is no standard mental health program in Paris beside the meter bar. The nature of the content and the order in which it is presented must be derived from such practical and theoretical knowledge as is available. Therefore, certain assumptions and certain organizing principles were elaborated before the detailed planning began.

Firstly, it was assumed that ignorance and fear with regard to mental illness were widespread. For this assumption there was thought to be sound empirical evidence, gathered by all members of the committee while either teaching student nurses or working with lay groups. The psychiatrists reported experiences of ignorance and fear while engaged in therapeutic work with patients or their families.

The committee members also pooled their impressions of nurses' attitudes toward mental illness. They agreed that the girls on the whole tended to think about mental illnesses as either behavior disorders caused by poor heredity or as moral disorders caused by weakness of character. While the committee members were aware of the biological and hereditary bases of mental illness, they believed there was also a causal connection with long-term disturbances of interpersonal relationships. They felt that acceptance of this fact would result in a greater tendency to consider the mentally ill unfortunate in their life situation and less tendency to view them as "bad" or of "inferior stock." Such a shift, they reasoned, would make rehabilitation easier.

Secondly, the planning committee assumed that there was a similarity between attitudes toward mental illness and prejudice against underprivileged groups. Because of prejudice against them, it is difficult to reintegrate people into communities once they have been designated mentally ill. Social workers with whom we have discussed the question say that one of their greatest problems lies in persuading patients' relatives, employers, and neighbors to receive them back; clinical experience with patients in group therapy has shown us how apprehensively they view approaching discharge, as if they anticipated something very similar to prejudice from their families and communities.

Our problem, therefore, seemed to the committee to share some elements with that of education for interracial tolerance. Williams[94] believes that prejudice and its concomitant "scapegoating" are usually the result of a projective mechanism in which one's own unacceptable impulses are ascribed to the scapegoat. He has, therefore, suggested that there is a danger in conducting unilateral educational programs directed at decreasing hostility toward one single minority group because they may succeed at the expense of actually raising prejudice toward some other group. If he is right, it is probable that negative feelings are to some extent transferred to some other object when they are reduced toward the mentally ill. Furthermore, many workers have reported difficulty in lowering the absolute level of prejudice in a population,[94, 22, 85, 72] whether or not it is redirected at another object.*

On the basis of the concept of the equilibrating function of prejudice for some people, we decided not to make a direct attack, at least at first, upon the attitudes of the members of our community toward the mentally ill but to approach by way of the more general subject of normal human behavior. Discussion of social distance from the mentally ill or social responsibility for the problem of mental illness, the two dimensions in which we were interested, would be left for later stages of the program. We hoped in this way to avoid some of the difficulties experienced by workers during attempts to lessen prejudice against minorities.

After considerable discussion, we agreed upon the following working principles as a starting point in the educational program:

(a) Behavior is caused and is therefore understandable and subject to change.

(b) There is a continuum between normality and abnormality.

(c) There is a wider variety of normal behavior than is generally realized.

At the time of planning the program, we felt that by em-

---

* The extensive empirical work in this area has tended to be socio-psychological in nature and problem-oriented, focusing on "who is prejudiced toward whom and under what circumstances." The results of this type of research were extremely helpful to us in the formulation of our program of education, enabling us to avoid certain mistakes, but our primary interest lay not so much in discovering the variables correlated with prejudice against the mentally ill as in discovering the mutability of this prejudice. Our focus might be said to be upon the attributes of the *norms themselves* rather than upon the attributes of the individuals who uphold them or depart from them.

phasizing these three principles it might be possible to nar-
row the distance between the mentally ill and the well, especially between those who return to the community from
a mental hospital and the community itself. We reasoned
that by teaching that there is little difference between illness
and health, we would persuade people to behave toward the
ill as they do toward the well.

The essential naiveté of our thinking at this stage will be
discussed in detail later.

In planning the *method* of education, as distinguished
from the *content,* the committee decided that mass media
should be used as little as possible, because their success in
changing opinions and attitudes is open to question.[53] The
type of material that we were trying to teach requires a
shifting of the accepted standards of groups of people,* and
therefore we felt that small group discussions led by people
skilled in dealing with mental health topics should be used
wherever possible.

However, we knew that although small group discussion
was considered by the committee to be the method of choice,
it was unrealistic to suppose that all adults in any community
would be willing to involve themselves in such discussions.
Therefore we were prepared to use certain of the mass media
when it seemed necessary for increasing the numbers of people affected. We anticipated that we would have to exploit
any opportunity in our attempt to educate this rather conservative community in a fairly sensitive subject.

2. *The Content*

We would like to make it very clear that we were not, in
this study, testing the efficacy of any particular type of educational material. Our purpose was to find out as best we

* Our thinking at this point had been influenced by Lewin's[48] work with
group norms, the reports of Alcoholics Anonymous groups, and the general
trend toward the use of the small group in education.

could whether the then current concepts and materials of the Mental Health Association and of the professional members of the psychiatric services would materially shift attitudes toward mental illness when taught to the best of our ability.

Education essentially began with the first entrance into the town. Our first stop was at a local store whose owner was an old acquaintance. To him we explained our interest in learning what the citizens of Blackfoot thought about mental illness and the mentally ill. During our discussion he posed a question—and we were to hear it repeated many times—"Why do you want to know what we think? Why not go to the experts? It's their business to know." To this we soon learned how to reply with a counter-question, "Who sends people to mental hospitals?" In answering this question, many people placed the responsibility on the local doctor, but we tried to develop the idea that the family and friends of a mentally ill person are those who take him to the doctor and ask that something be done. We told our friend the storekeeper that many experts feel that some of the patients in mental hospitals are no more ill than others who remain harmlessly in the community and that this is because community beliefs and attitudes differ from one place to another and from one situation to another.

From this contact in the town, we moved outward. Our friend supplied us with the names of all of the people whom he considered to be leaders in the community. The list included not only town officials but many executive officers of local clubs and organizations. Over a period of about a week we called on each of these. We talked about our survey, asked for permission to attend their club meetings from time to time, and volunteered, when it seemed appropriate, to help in the planning of some of their winter programs. Their response was friendly, polite, and perhaps somewhat puzzled. They certainly seemed to understand the intellectual content of our purpose but they had trouble understanding our motivation. This type of research is, after all, considered a normal occupation by very few people!

When our initial rounds were completed, we had a chat with the proprietor of the local weekly newspaper and gave him a release concerning our program. He promised to cooperate and in the months that followed gave us considerable assistance. News stories and articles which we furnished appeared in his paper almost every week. In addition we bought advertising space to publicize various facets of our program. This editor also gave us editorial support on several occasions.

People had various reasons for being interested in our presence in town. The mayor, for instance, was a man who had gained national prominence in curling and baseball. As a sportsman he had no interest in mental health, psychiatrists, or research, but in his official role he made it his business to find out that we had respectable backing and meant no harm to the community. His interest then left us and returned to his major preoccupations. This investigative quality was characteristic of many of our initial contacts.

Despite the fact that we were pushed by the self-imposed time limits of our program, we tried to proceed slowly and to let our informal meetings with the townsfolk open the way gradually for activities that would be mutually helpful. Not all of our contacts had direct consequences for our program. One incident would perhaps typify a number. In the early days of the program we called upon the public school principal to tell him of our purpose in the town and to inform him that we had been discussing a winter program with the P.T.A. He informed us in no uncertain terms that he considered any P.T.A. an unnecessary nuisance and that his opinion of "psychology" was very low. Despite this we continued to work with the P.T.A. and as the winter progressed we came to respect this man both for his forthrightness and for his intelligence. He was an authority on local history and was very much interested in a local historical society. Before the winter was out we were on close enough terms with him that when we were about to cooperate with the historical society by providing prizes for an essay contest on the subject of the pioneer days of the district, he consented to be the chief judge while one of us acted as another judge. (Through these essays we were able to learn a good deal about the historical background of the community.) The relationship between the education director and the school teacher at the end of the program was one of friendship and mutual respect, although each no doubt considered the other misguided.

The effect of activities, such as the judging of the essay contest, which were peripheral to our main purpose is very hard to judge. Many times the conversation on coffee row, in someone's kitchen, or in the Legion clubroom turned to mental illness because this was what we were associated with, and we feel that these chats must have had an effect. What this effect might have been will be discussed in a later section. We have happy memories of these relationships which we enjoyed in Blackfoot.

During all of our contacts, formal and informal, with the citizens of Blackfoot we stressed our desire to know their thoughts about mental health and mental illness in order that general knowledge of the subject might be enlarged. At all times we emphasized that the lack of an undivided body of expert opinion available on the subject made everyone's opinion valuable.

To those who are familiar with more elaborate community studies and the methods which have been used to enter communities in such projects, this straightforward approach may seem both foolhardy and naive. Some investigators feel that one must live in a town for at least a year before being ready to begin on a program of this sort; some feel that the formation of local advisory committees is an essential first step; and still others think that signs of local interest must precede any such program. These restrictions are not, however, totally relevant in this particular case. Interest in mental health was at the time widespread in Prairie Province. As we have mentioned earlier, the professional staff of the Psychiatric Service had, at that time, many demands for information, talks, films, etc. In fact, as we have since come to realize, many of our psychiatrists, while not considering mental health education to be part of their work, were busier dealing with requests for this sort of service than some of their counterparts in projects explicitly devoted to such education. There is good evidence that a general interest in the subject existed, even though specific requests had not been made from Blackfoot.

The principal investigator, who had spent his childhood and youth within 100 miles of Blackfoot, could however name only two friends in the town before he entered the community. On the other hand, he knew that it would be similar to many prairie communities in which he had lived. He knew, too, that as soon as he had begun to talk to local people, he would find that he had a host of shared friends and acquaintances from college days, from the Armed Forces, and from the people he knew in Prairie City, where he had attended high school. This was indeed so, and Blackfoot was in no sense foreign to us when we began our study.

Local advisory boards do have a function in programs such as ours, but in this area they might have a strained, "imported" flavor. Blackfoot people go to political meetings, farm forum meetings, health education meetings, and many other sorts of gatherings which originate outside their community. They are not suspicious of outsiders, especially when they are, as we were, scarcely outsiders at all. For example, during the course of our experiment, an outside effort to incorporate the town of Blackfoot into a larger public health unit was made. The proponents of the scheme, Provincial civil servants, entered the community with considerably more directness than we did; they distributed literature, hired a hall, and when the people came, told them about the plan. Blackfoot people argued with the proponents of the scheme, but they listened, and when the matter came to a vote, the town, which had seemed completely opposed to a change, voted for the formation of such a health unit.

We might call our approach to Blackfoot "native." We went in as fellow-citizens of Prairie Province with a long experience in very similar communities, with shared friends and acquaintances, and with much shared experience, and we approached the people of Blackfoot with methods which were in their—and our—own tradition.

The introduction into the town of a questionnaire and an interview—the "pre-" of our pre- and post-test design—created a good deal of discussion; many respondents expressed some curiosity about the general subject, and some expressed a polite interest in the program to follow. This interest was partly created by a front-page story in the local weekly newspaper explaining the sponsorship of the research and pointing out that this was not a "case-finding" program.* There was no incident during the initial measurement of attitudes or during the gathering of the interview data that impressed any member of the research team as being exceptional in any way. The weather was fine, the people seemed friendly, and morale among the interviewers and researchers was high.

---

* Actually, the editor spontaneously wrote a short editorial to this effect after hearing comments such as "They must think we're nuts"; the interviewers stressed the same point.

The first group with whom the team worked was the recently organized and still unstable Parent-Teacher Association. An offer to schedule a winter program for this group was gratefully accepted by the executive. Professional members of the staffs of the Psychiatric Service Department, the Adult Education Department, and the School Psychologists' Division of the Department of Education were invited to address the P.T.A. on a variety of subjects. For example, one member of the Department of Education spoke on the role of the school in developing the personality of the child, and his talk was followed by an animated discussion of certain specific practical problems.

Later in the year a weekly radio program sponsored by the P.T.A. and financed and administered by the project was presented over a twelve-week period. Known as "Junior Jury," this program consisted in panel discussions of problems of childhood, discussed first by a group of children, then by a group of parents, and finally by a psychiatrist who summarized the discussion. Most problems were submitted by the school children themselves and presumably arose out of their life situations. Typical questions dealt with sibling rivalry, with authority relationships with parents, and with the degree of autonomy a child should have regarding money and property. A telephone check made one evening half way through the series found 60 per cent of radio listeners tuned to the program.

The P.T.A. undertook upon our suggestion to sponsor a three-day "film festival" consisting of mental health films of various sorts, concerned mainly with the mechanisms of behavior, but varied with artistic and documentary films. A total of 260 people attended this festival, and, in all, 60 stayed to form small discussion groups afterward. Films included such well-known titles as *The Quiet One, Children's Play,* and *Human Beginnings.*

It should not be felt that the P.T.A., because it was new and still unstable, was a deviant organization. Its instability stemmed from two sources: it was very new, having been formed only the year before, and it was opposed by the school principal, a firm individualist nearing retirement, who felt that schooling was the province of school teachers and should not be invaded by parents. It is certain that the executive's difficult task of putting this organization on a firm basis was part of the reason for the warm welcome which it gave us. Moreover, there is probably no other community organization which has so much common interest with a mental health educator as a P.T.A. The P.T.A. did a great deal for our program. On the other hand we feel that our program and our staff did a great deal to strengthen the P.T.A. and that it was in a stronger position when we left it than when we came.

Through the cooperation of the principal of the high school it was possible to provide a speaker for the local Teachers' Convention. He discussed the relationship of different methods of teaching to personality development. Later a series of five meetings with the older high school students was arranged; discussions centered in the subject of occupational choice, but extended at times to the allied topics of causes of behavior, behavior in situations where choices were hard to make, and problems of adapting to an adult role in the occupational world. Discussion was animated at these meetings, and the students said that they enjoyed them.

A certain amount of education was done through the local newspaper, whose cooperative editor reported weekly news of our program. From time to time we bought space to advertise meetings and editorialize on the subject of mental health. For example, we inserted summary discussions of the topics raised on the "Junior Jury" radio program.

Pamphlets on mental health topics were placed on display

in public buildings, and they could be had by mailing a coupon cut from the newspaper. Despite this advertising, however, distribution was very restricted, while, on the other hand, certain books placed in the Public Library were taken out frequently. These included such works as *You and Psychiatry*, by Menninger and Leaf; *Alcohol, One Man's Meat*, by Strecker and Chambers; and other books written for the layman about psychiatry. The Library Board came to the perhaps not surprising decision that these books should be dealt with in the same way as those donated by evangelical religious groups such as Jehovah's Witnesses, and therefore a limit was placed upon the number which the Library could accept. In spite of this restriction, or perhaps because of it, the books enjoyed good circulation. We do not know, however, who took the books out, and it is possible that they were not read as frequently as the circulation indicated.*

Early in the autumn, under the leadership of a psychiatrist, a study group was formed for people interested in nontechnical discussions of human behavior. This group started with 5 members and increased to 35. The members discussed the mechanisms of normal personality, saw illustrative films, and toward the end discussed the neuroses and the functional psychoses. Like all other groups with which we became familiar in Blackfoot this one had a changing population; people attended a few meetings, dropped out, and were replaced by others. The peak membership of 35 under-represents, therefore, the total number involved in this group at one time or another.

During the early part of the program, a request was received for a speaker for the Civil Servants' Association, and a film called *Breakdown,* made by the National Film Board

---

* A recent article by Granville Hicks in *The American Scholar* discusses reading patterns in a small New England town. He recognizes a small class of omnivorous readers, and perhaps Blackfoot has such a group, who read whatever appears on the shelf.

of Canada and widely used for teaching all over Canada and the United States, was taken to the meeting. This film, which is extremely dramatic, had been assessed by us some time earlier at its Canadian première, and analysis of questionnaires completed at that time by a randomly selected audience had indicated that in spite of being artistic and convincing, it had left the audience anxious and dismayed. The main reason for this dismay seemed to have been the lack of "cause" for a sudden dramatic schizophrenic breakdown suffered by the heroine of the film, a young woman of twenty-three. Investigation revealed that the makers of the picture had thought the etiology of the disease, or at least the precipitating circumstances, to be implicit in the story, but the responses of the audience had shown plainly that this was not so for most people.

In spite of the results of this assessment, the film was used in Blackfoot because it was in frequent use by the Mental Health Association and because the small group discussion method was expected to elucidate the "cause" of the breakdown and thus relieve anxiety. About 30 people viewed the film, and for about an hour and a half afterward they discussed it in groups of 10, each with a psychiatrist or psychiatric social worker leading the discussion. The leaders reported immediately afterward that the film seemed to raise anxiety but that this anxiety had been "talked out" and "worked through" in the discussion. Nevertheless, this group voted at its next meeting to have no more mental health speakers or films, and in doing so reversed a previous decision to invite a series of speakers. A discussion of this action will follow in the next chapter, but it is worth noting in passing that our assumption that the small group discussion method would effectively handle anxieties raised by the nature of the educational material appears to have been wrong.

Shortly after this event, we received a request for a study

group leader from a number of young married couples who wished instruction in the emotional aspects of the care of infants and children. This discussion group, led by a psychiatrist from a guidance clinic, met a total of six times and the leader declared it a satisfactory experience from his point of view. The program consisted of films and talks. The focus for discussion was the personality of the small child and the effect of different kinds of parental treatment in forming this personality.

A public debate on the subject of whether or not social science is really a science was arranged with the agricultural station group. Although this debate was rather lively in a somewhat incoherent way, it seemed amiable enough; therefore we were surprised to learn from acquaintances that it had raised considerable antagonism among the agricultural scientists present. In content, the discussion seemed innocuous; the speakers for the social science side emphasized the contributions of R. A. Fisher to the art of experimental design, and the agriculturalists insisted that "man is too complicated to be studied scientifically." Which aspects of the debate annoyed the agriculturalists most is still in doubt, though we will suggest in a later section that it was not the content of the debate but the fact of the educational team, by their actions, implicitly calling themselves scientists which was so vexatious.

Upon their own request 90 members of the Blackfoot Board of Trade were addressed on the subject of the psychiatric services of the Province; the talk was essentially a plea for more public interest in the problems of two overcrowded mental hospitals, and it was politely received by this large audience.

Probably the most successful event of the program was the engagement of several members of the Blackfoot Branch of the Canadian Legion in a project which took them seventy-five miles to visit a veterans group in a ward of a large mental hospital. These men were given a one-hour introduction to the problem of the chronic ward by the superintendent, and following this they visited the patients. The Legion members voted at their next meeting to adopt this ward as a continuing project, sending cigarettes, candies, and other comforts. It is of particular interest that this Legion group decided not to limit its interest to the veterans when sending comforts to the ward but to include the whole ward in its project. Apparently the governing Legion principle of service to veterans was temporarily replaced by a broader interest in all the patients in the hospital.

3. *The Coverage and Method*

We do not definitely know how many of the people of Blackfoot were touched by our educational program. Certainly the radio program, newspaper articles, and the film festival were *available* to the whole community. On the other hand, many of the one-evening events were conducted under the sponsorship of various clubs, and since the membership of most of these societies in Blackfoot is overlapping, many items of the program involved a limited group. No work was done with church groups because we felt it unwise to be identified with any one church and we were unable to gain the cooperation of the local Roman Catholic priest, even though we had received an assurance from the Archbishop of the diocese that the Church had no official objection to the program. At the time of the resurvey, 56 per cent of the people interviewed had had some contact with the program and were aware of its content, but these people were concentrated in the upper and medium rental areas. Apparently our methods were inadequate for reaching the lower rental area residents, and no doubt Kingsley Davis' interpretation[17] of the middle-class orientation of mental health educators is particularly relevant here. His suggestion that middle-class people join the mental health movement and proceed to teach middle-class values as mental health principles is probably true of our workers, who were middle-class in their personal orientation and who certainly attracted middle-class audiences. Until the resurvey, we could not be sure how far our program was reaching. We were certainly not being heard by the Métis, in the lowest social class, but we could think of no way of reaching them except through the Catholic Church, and this avenue was closed to us. We were furthermore faced with a dilemma; the more we tried to reach all social classes, the more we would deviate from typical mental health education programs which are aimed at and demanded by the middle class. We compromised by using all avenues which were open to us, using the techniques and materials available.

Apparently somewhat over one-half of the Blackfoot people, mostly living in the middle and upper rental areas, were aware of our educational program.* The material of the program, in the form of talks, films, and radio programs, ranged from infant care to the nature of the functional psychoses; "the causes of human behavior" was the common theme. The following list indicates the type of material used and gives an estimate of the number of people upon whom it impinged.

(a) There were about 40 adults with each of whom we had more than 20 contacts. They helped organize meetings, participated in radio broadcasts, and worked with us closely. With them we had numerous informal social meetings, and we came to know them all.

(b) Approximately 160 people attended a series of meet-

* This estimate was made by the interviewers, who asked their respondents, during the second survey, what parts of the program they were familiar with.

ings or showed sporadic interest in several parts of the project. The research team knew most of them by name. They had contact with the project in situations where it was possible to have discussion with them, and their contacts numbered between 5 and 20.

(c) Nearly 400 people came to between 1 and 5 meetings organized by the project. Mostly these were contacts in which there was no discussion—large meetings, or small meetings without discussion. Many of these persons' names would be unfamiliar to us.

(d) A further group of unknown size listened to the radio programs, read newspaper stories and columns, took books which we supplied from the library, or saw films which we sponsored. Many of them must have discussed the program informally, but we have no way of measuring their participation.

We tried during all of these activities not to oversell our program, to encourage local participation, and to avoid antagonizing people. Within the limits imposed by the total time available, we almost always let the townspeople make the pace; occasionally in the beginning we even had to act as a restraining influence upon our more enthusiastic supporters.

Our entry into the town, as we have said before, was through a friend. In order to gain acceptance, the early days of the experiment were spent in meeting and talking with key persons in the more prominent organizations in the town; because of multiple membership this was not a formidable task. Our contacts were informal; we drank many cups of coffee, chatted in stores during slack periods, went to meetings of various organizations when we were invited, and on cold days warmed our feet at the coal stove in a local service station. We tried to be sensitive to the feelings of the townsfolk, and yet to remember the principle developed by anthropologists that the first person who will espouse a new idea will be someone who is partially deviant in his own group. Fortunately for our purposes, the local P.T.A., only a year old, was struggling to keep alive and to maintain the interest of the parents in the public school and its problems. A natural similarity of interests led the executive of this organization and our educators together, and this was a most fruitful and friendly association.

At all times we tried not to imply that we wished to organize Blackfoot's activities; in fact in the majority of cases we provided the materials and the local people did the organizing.

The total influence of this program is, of course, unknown, but there are two effects which we can describe: the shift in attitudes as measured by our scales, and the level of anxiety which our efforts created in Blackfoot. The analysis of the scale results will be discussed later; we will now turn to a consideration of the manifest anxiety and hostility generated by our program.

The Community Reaction
to the Program

1. *The Events*

The reaction of the townsfolk to the educational program and to the periods of interviewing which preceded and followed it can be described in a narrative which begins with our initial reception into the town when we first talked with prominent local people and found them polite, interested, and if not exactly enthusiastic, at least cooperative and willing to accept our program on trial. We were able to enlist the help of about 15 people from three different organizations to assist in distributing and collecting questionnaires from house to house. It is interesting that these people volunteered for an onerous and rather thankless task without any great pressure being put upon them.

This benign atmosphere of cooperation continued during the week in which a six-person team lived in the community and carried on their 100 interviews. Later they reported that although the town was conservative, it was essentially friendly. They met with relatively few refusals and their general reception was such that they enjoyed their work. The respondents joked pleasantly with the interviewers and in general performed the role of good hosts. As the weeks proceeded, however, we found that we could arouse little *active* interest in the program, although the friendliness of the citizens seemed unchanged. As this indifferent courtesy continued, the concern of the educational team became high; and they feared they would never get sufficient enthusiasm in the community to enable them to sponsor an educational program at all!

In the fourth week of the program, when certain activities such as the winter program for the P.T.A. had finally been arranged, two rumors cut a swath through the town and came to us from several sources. The first was to the effect that "the Government" had sent out this research team to investigate attitudes toward mental illness in Blackfoot because "they" were thinking of building a new mental hospital there. On the surface, this rumor is not unreasonable because the content of the early interviews and questionnaires was such as to make this conclusion quite feasible. In spite of being logical, however, this rumor was not grounded in any facts which we could discover. Discussion of building a new mental hospital is endemic in Prairie Province, but no recent event had suggested anything more. When this not unreasonable rumor died out, another and truly bizarre one took its place. It was said that the survey was a "plot" of the Roman Catholic Church. Although the Roman Catholic clergy had expressed approval of our program at its higher levels, the Blackfoot parish priest, whose flock amounts to 10 or 15 per cent of the population, had been completely uncooperative. He declared that statements which had been made by Mental Health Association officials in British Columbia and in Quebec had seemed to him to be anti-religious.

A visit to the Archbishop of the Diocese reassured us that there was no formal objection to our program but at the same time made it plain that no pressure would be brought to bear upon the priest in Blackfoot to secure his coopera- tion. To sum up, our relationship with the church was some- where between cool and cordial, but a small amount of in- vestigation would most certainly have revealed that the church was very far from having anything to do with our program. The only connection between this rumor and real- ity that we could discover was the coincidental membership of a P.T.A. executive member in the Roman Catholic Church. It will be recalled that the P.T.A. was our first con- tact in the town.

At the time we interpreted these rumors as an effort of the citizens of Blackfoot to explain, more satisfactorily than we had been able to, our presence in the town. Apparently our reasons published in the weekly newspaper (that Black- foot was typical of a certain section of the Province, and that it was well known for the cooperativeness of its citi- zenry) were unconvincing.

Before Christmas, three months after the program had started, we began to notice a pattern of withdrawing be- havior which was to become increasingly familiar. There had been, for example, a rapid turnover of members in the small study group, the most enthusiastically involved of all the groups with which we worked. At the time we thought that in this highly overorganized town, with its many activi- ties, other claims upon people's attention were causing this defection from the study group; that was the reason people gave us.

Similarly, attendance at the P.T.A. rotated as the year went by, and again an interpretation of "other interests" was made. Hundreds of casual remarks led us to believe that a falling off of attendance toward the end of the year was directly caused by an upswing of competing activities. "People say there's nothing to do in Blackfoot but you could keep going morning, noon, and night if you belonged to everything," we were told. Much later, and with hindsight, we suspected that it was the frequency of people's remarks concerning the pressure of community activities which had increased rather than the number of activities themselves!

Again, all who attended the Film Festival were urged to stay for discussion afterward, but less than one quarter did so. The dramatic refusal of the Civil Servants' Association to see any further mental health films after the showing of *Breakdown* has been described previously. It will be recalled that they had originally intended to see a series of such films, but were dissuaded from doing so by this first experience.

Toward the end of the program we were beginning to feel that there was something very wrong. Among other things, the psychiatrist who headed the educational program was beginning to feel increasingly reluctant to travel to the community, although he was at a loss to explain this feeling, especially as he had experienced no overt rudeness or rejection in the town.

In the late winter, a local woman from whom we had received much helpful cooperation warned us several times that we would be wise to stop certain activities, as they had "run their course." This woman had displayed enthusiasm for our project in the autumn because of her own interest in planning a winter program for the P.T.A., which she had been active in organizing. She was an intelligent, alert woman, with a number of relatives and friends in town, and so far as we could judge, not one of the "marginal" people who the anthropologists warn us can be expected to join the ranks of a new movement in a small community. Nevertheless, she displayed considerable anxiety about our continued presence in the town, in spite of her original helpful enthusiasm, and she continued to do so until the end of the experiment.

Perhaps the most revealing single comment on the total community reaction was made by a man of considerable means and of great influence in the community. He knew of the project, but had not taken any active part in the program and was therefore somewhat vague as to its content. He said to an interviewer, "You've sure got this town by its ear," and went on to express at some length his amazement at the extent of the excitement and anger in the community. This was the first time it was said in so many words that our program was causing both anxiety and hostility. It should be emphasized that this man had not been in actual contact with the program but was aware only that it had something to do with mental illness. He had obviously not been subject to the same sorts of stimuli as had many of those who displayed hostility.

When the interviewing team arrived in Blackfoot to conduct the second survey, they were met with a type of behavior which had been absent the first time. They had scarcely arrived when the wife of one of the original members of the study group telephoned to say that she did not wish to be interviewed; she refused to give any reason for her request, nor did she explain why she thought she had been chosen for interviewing. She was reassured that if she did not wish it she would not be asked for an interview. Shortly afterward her husband telephoned to tell us that he also wished not to be interviewed and although he was in turn reassured, ten minutes later he presented himself in considerable agitation and said abruptly, "Withdraw my name from anything you have it on." One of us replied, "Certainly, but why?" and he replied, "There's no reason, I am just not interested, just put it that way, I'm just not interested," and with this he took his leave. As far as we could discover through subsequent queries, this man had been antagonized on the evening of the debate regarding the validity of social science. We could never find out what elements of this debate—which, as we have noted had been a lively but somewhat shapeless affair—had angered him, but in the light of his early association with the study group we are inclined to think his hostility was aroused by our effort, implicit in the debate, to legitimize our activities in the name of science.

During their week in the field during the resurvey, interviewers grew increasingly tense; they complained that their reception was cold and at times outright hostile. As they returned, we interviewed them. They all emphasized the discomfort of this second field experience, especially as contrasted with the first survey in the autumn. (The six people who conducted the first series of interviews, all of whom were experienced psychologists and social workers, expressed their willingness to repeat this task in the spring and four of them did so; the other two were out of the Province by spring.) Typical excerpts from the interviewers follow:

Interviewer 1: "Last time the people were either friendly or indifferent. This time out-and-out hostility, though I don't know whom it was towards. I had this feeling both from the people I interviewed and the refusals. . . . We felt hostility in the hotel the first day, unlike the first time, when we had an enjoyable stay, and in the cafe we had the feeling that people were talking about us."

Interviewer 2: This interviewer complained that compared with last time there was a terrible feeling that something was expected of him: ". . . I felt fear and hostility. . . . I had the feeling that the educational program had been felt by very many even though they had not a very clear idea what it was about . . . last time the jokes were about 'Blackfoot must be all crazy'; no jokes this time. The interviews were much quicker this time because I was afraid to probe. Even the cooperative people would ask, 'What do you want of us, anyway?' I felt everyone was suspicious."

Interviewer 3 said it was much worse than the first time. "The first time they were all curious, this time they were anxious. . . . They were afraid of anything about them being put down on paper. . . . They were afraid we had selected the sample for some reason. . . . They all seemed to be trying to get the interview over with . . . I was afraid to probe very far . . . I had the feeling that people were talking about the team and I was afraid to laugh in the restaurant for fear they would think we were laughing about them."

Interviewer 4, who was not on the first survey team, said "There were feelings of hostility coming through from people on the streets and in the restaurants and hotel; I felt we were being talked about. I felt a lot of anxiety floating around. . . . I only met three or four people who looked upon the survey as useful. . . ."

Interviewer 5: This interviewer was not on the first survey, and because he had been borrowed from a psychiatric clinic staff in another town, he caught a train for home before he could be interviewed. However, he complied with a request that he write a letter describing his experience; the following is an excerpt. "Regarding the main source of hostility, I would think it was basically in the population's own ignorance of mental illness. Over a period of years mental illness has been a taboo subject that was only whispered about. When people are shaken out of the ruts of their rigid trains of thought in which they can function with the least anxiety, hostility is naturally directed towards those who have upset these folkways. There has always been an aura of horror which surrounds the idea of insanity. Scarcely anything is more terrible to the ordinary person than the complete unpredictability of those who are mentally disordered.

The social milieu is based on predictability. The individual's own assurance, his security, his sense of his own reality are menaced by the spectacle of mental illness."

Interviewer 6: "Last time everyone was so friendly; this time they all tried to avoid us. . . . Last time we had so much fun going over the day with the others in the evening; this time we were too tense and miserable."

The descriptions above are specially selected to show the unanimity of opinion among the interviewers about how they felt in general in the town. At the same time two interviewers did say that they had encountered a few respondents who were enthusiastic about the program and found it very beneficial, but both considered these citizens to be confused in their ideas of what had been taught. For example, one of the more enthusiastic respondents told the interviewer that he had never realized that masturbation could cause mental illness until the psychiatrist had said that it could at one of the study group meetings. Upon investigation it transpired that the psychiatrist, who remembered the incident well, had said in reply to a question that the main danger in masturbation resides in the anxiety and guilt which it engenders and that this anxiety and guilt might be related to subsequent mental illness. He recalled emphasizing this point carefully because he feared the type of misunderstanding which seems to have occurred despite his effort. Possibly even the enthusiasts were essentially ambivalent to the project, and this respondent may have been unconsciously motivated to opposing the program.

Further evidence of this sort of misunderstanding lies in the spontaneous comment written across the bottom of one resurvey questionnaire: "These questions are impossible to answer coherently. Answers would depend upon mental patients in question. I would fear an ex-patient who had committed murder or a serious sex crime, but I would not fear one who had been docile or merely suffered hallucinations or other mild forms of insanity." This respondent was in the medium education category, in a medium rental area, and aged between twenty and forty years. His response to the question, "What sort of man is really respected in this community?" was classified in the most popular category. In short, this was an average citizen in terms of our categories, and with his manifest lack of ability to discriminate between mild and serious forms of insanity and his tendency to associate mental illness with sex crimes and murder makes us count him a failure from the point of view of our program. His comment, quoted above, is doubly interesting because he makes a very intelligent criticism of the scale items.

The event which best symbolizes our hostile rejection by Blackfoot occurred during the course of the second survey when the Mayor of the town approached one of our interviewers, asked him what he was doing, questioned him in great detail about his credentials and his right to conduct such interviews, and finally said, "We have had too much of this sort of thing; we are not interested in it in this town any more. The sooner you leave, the better." The ranks had closed against us; Blackfoot had responded as if to a threat to its integrity as a functioning community.

2. *The Interpretation of the Events*

The distress of our interviewers demonstrated dramatically the anxiety we had produced in Blackfoot. In large part the educators failed to recognize this anxiety* until late in the program, but it may perhaps be inferred from three types of responses:

---

* Sullivan[88] has said that anxiety is specifically a response to any threat to a valued interpersonal relationship, and it is in his sense that we use the term. We take the social system as a frame of reference and regard the anxiety as the response to a threat to stable social integration, that is to reliable interpersonal relationships.

(a) An aggressive or hostile response.
(b) A removal or flight response.
(c) Probably the response of apathy, which may be a special case of flight.

In the nature of the case, it is difficult to see a removal response unless it is a sufficiently obvious or total removal to call attention to itself. Apathy, however, is visible. While it was present from the beginning in Blackfoot, it was at first interpreted, not as anxiety, but rather as a function of the conservatism of the town and as that perfectly natural lack of interest and involvement in our program which might be termed the "inertia of the system." It was manifested by a reserved politeness, present when we first entered the town and persistent until just at the end.

The two rumors concerning the building of a new mental hospital and the clerical plot were interpreted at the time that they occurred as attempts to rationalize our presence in the community, but in retrospect, it seems more reasonable to consider them as anxiety reactions.

Before Christmas, withdrawal and flight reactions were taking place, although at the time we did not interpret them as such. One of the flight patterns which we did not recognize is described in detail above: the rapid turnover of participants in the activities sponsored by the educational team. The study group member who demonstrated his hostility in a personal visit to the interviewers is probably the most striking example of overt hostility.

The failure of the team to recognize this withdrawing response is pointed up by the experience with the cooperative woman who originally worked with us but later became disturbed and anxious because we would not terminate certain activities, among them the study group. Entirely apart from any conflicts within her personality which may have been relevant, she was, after all, closely identified with the research project, and there seems to be little doubt that she was sensitive both to the mounting hostility among her friends and acquaintances toward the project, and to her own increasing isolation from them because of her role as our ally. She would undoubtedly have liked to tell us that it was time to pull out altogether, but being unable to verbalize her intuitive feelings about the mood of the community, she was only able to say that she thought it was time to stop certain activities because they seemed to have "run their course" or because "everyone is so busy at other things." There is evidence from the interviewers that some of her friends were indeed annoyed with her for her identification with the program and for her symbolic betrayal of her town in its resistance to the educators.

Finally the Mayor's request that we leave the town as soon as possible climaxed the expression of rejection of the town toward the team. This episode, coming as it did close to the end of our stay, seemed a ritualistic affirmation of the solidarity of the town against us. The Mayor was, after all, not himself an aggressive man; we were convinced that he was playing a truly representative role at this moment . . . he spoke for Blackfoot.

Generally speaking, we believe Blackfoot's response to our mental health educational program was that of anxiety. This anxiety was first manifested as apathy, continued as withdrawal, and finally culminated in hostility and aggression at the verbal level. Further empirical evidence that something had gone very wrong with our relationship to Blackfoot citizens resides in the fact that the second survey yielded 100 fewer questionnaires than the first, even though the method of collection was replicated as closely as possible.* The dropping off of respondents cut across both age and education.

As well as the loss of numbers of questionnaires, the sec-

---

* In Deerville, 107 questionnaires were obtained each time, and no attempts were made to get total coverage.

ond survey yielded fewer data regarding age and education, and fewer people signed their names, as Tables 1 and 2 show. All these differences are great enough to warrant their interpretation as caused by something other than chance.

TABLE 1. Willingness to Give Signatures*

Blackfoot—First and Second Questionnaires

	RESPONDENTS				
	First quest.		Second quest.		Total no.
	No.	%	No.	%	
Names signed	173	(32)	89	(20)	263
Names not signed	367	(68)	349	(80)	715
Total	540	(100)	438	(100)	978

$$\chi^2 = 16.93$$
$$P < .001$$

* A space for signature was provided on the questionnaires, but beneath this space appeared the sentence, "You need not sign your name unless you wish to."

TABLE 2. Willingness to Give Information about Age and/or Education

Blackfoot—First and Second Questionnaires

	RESPONDENTS				
	First quest.		Second quest.		Total no.
	No.	%	No.	%	
Information withheld	33	(6)	46	(10)	79
Information given	507	(94)	392	(90)	899
Total	540	(100)	438	(100)	978

$$\chi^2 = 5.70$$
$$.02 > P > .01$$

There remains the problem of being certain of exactly what caused the anxiety. As the aggression was directed against the almost unknown interviewers and not against the educators, we feel justified in believing that it was not simply personal animosity. Furthermore, the interviewers reported a radical difference between survey and resurvey, so that it could hardly have been the interview or questionnaire material. We believe it was the content and method of presentation of the material; although, lacking an independent evaluation of this all-important side-effect, we cannot be sure.

Three months after the final survey, the authors accepted the invitation of a Blackfoot friend to visit the town on the day of the celebration of the fiftieth anniversary of its incorporation. This gay event, with its long and elaborate parade, gave evidence of active and enthusiastic cooperation and organization on the part of large numbers of people. We were greeted with great friendliness by all we met. They asked us the rhetorical question, "How do you like our Golden Jubilee Celebration?" and their geniality was perhaps a reflection of their satisfaction with the fact that the same community integration which had so effectively closed ranks through apathy, withdrawal, and hostility had made this elaborate ritual demonstration of solidarity possible.

Part II

The Empirical Analysis

The Measurement of Results

1. *Collection of the Data*

Many Blackfoot citizens were involved in the distribution of our initial questionnaire. Through appeals to organizations, the chairman of our education committee was able to arrange to have the forms distributed by a group of local people. We felt that they were very eager to be active in their roles as organization members, and that their cooperation arose from enthusiasm for a "project" rather than from any particular interest in the subject.

These voluntary canvassers delivered to each household, at about four o'clock one September afternoon, a questionnaire for each adult member. Each canvasser asked that it be filled in immediately and given back to him when he returned after the evening meal.

We felt it important that there should be no time for people to discuss the meaning of the questionnaires. This is not the sort of subject upon which people usually reflect, and, furthermore, the statements are of such a degree of unsophistication that any serious contemplation of them makes one realize that there are a good number of contingencies which could affect the answers—indeed, a few respondents pointed this out. What we wanted was the immediate, spontaneous response, and we believed that this would be jeopardized by any degree of reflection. *In particular we did not want the respondents to make objective examinations and comparisons of the meaning of the term "mental illness" with one another, wishing rather that they should respond as they ordinarily would to these words.* The interviewers picked up the questionnaires immediately after supper whether or not they were complete and in this way ensured a minimum of discussion between households. On the other hand, a large number of questionnaires were lost through the absence of adult members from home during the short interval when the questionnaires were available.

A total of 560 people returned the questionnaires. Of these, 540 had answered more than half of the questions; the remaining questionnaires were rejected. This group of 540 respondents represents about 60 per cent of the adult residents of Blackfoot. It is not possible to be more precise because we do not know for certain how many permanent residents were in Blackfoot at the time of the survey. Many of its citizens are farmers who make frequent trips back and forth from farm to town. Some have residences in both places, and some leave the community for extended trips in the off-season, while a further group maintain a technical residence in Blackfoot but are, in fact, absentee landlords. Of our 540 questionnaires, 520 contained the ages of the respondents, and the distribution of these did not differ from the ages of the total population of the town as recorded by the Dominion Bureau of the Census.

Because of the double-residence habit of some farmers,

---

* It will be recalled that we were investigating the range of meanings assigned to this term by means of an intensive interview.

we planned to enter the community immediately upon the conclusion of fall harvesting. However, extraordinarily rainy weather and a late crop season meant that many people were still on the land. If we were to await the conclusion of all harvesting operations we would cut into the length of the educational program, because the same problems of farm activity and weather would control the time of the second survey in the spring. We do not know how many people were actually present in the town at the time of the survey, nor do we know what sorts of people, other than some farmers, are lost from our sample, although it may well be that the wealthier group is underrepresented because of a direct relationship between land-owning and wealth. All we can unequivocally say is that our 540 respondents represent about 60 per cent of the adult members of the community.

2. *The Scales*

The 23 items used in the questionnaire were analyzed, by Guttman's method, for "scalability." This means that they were tested to see if the items all lay upon one dimension. The items yielded two scales, indicating that we were tapping two dimensions, one of which we called "social distance," containing 8 items, and one of which we called "social responsibility," containing 4.

These names are somewhat arbitrary, since the meaning of the Guttman scales had to be inferred from the items which "scaled." The very fact that they scaled at all means technically that the attitudes tapped are unidimensional and not a mixture of a number of related attitudes. The investigator must sometimes interpret the content of each attitude dimension from those questions which remain in the scale, those which fall out in the scaling process, and from his experience with the test under various situations. In our case, the original set of items was thought to be a single dimension of "constructive" versus "non-constructive" attitudes toward mental illness, and the two scales were not evident to us until after the scaling process was completed. A detailed account of this scaling process with a description of the non-scaling items appears in Appendix I.

The assignment of the name "social distance" to the first of our scales is relatively straightforward, and we think this scale indicates how close a relationship the respondent is prepared to tolerate with someone who has been mentally ill.

"Social responsibility" is less straightforward because it covers two possible ideas: responsibility for causing illness, as well as responsibility for assuming the social burden which the mentally ill person places on society. At the time that we were setting up the questionnaire items we in fact meant "responsibility for causation," and there is some evidence, discussed in Appendix I, that this is the meaning that our respondents assigned to the questions. However, there is other evidence that some of them assigned the alternative meaning—responsibility for care of the mentally ill—to all the items, and this too is discussed in Appendix I. However, as the attitude is at least technically unidimensional, we will proceed on the assumption that there is a single more general meaning in all of these items which includes both of the specific meanings we have described. This assumption can of course be tested in the future and demonstrated to be right or wrong, but for the purposes of the rest of this book we shall use the term *social responsibility* to refer to this more general attitude unless we state explicitly that we are referring to one of the specific attitudes—responsibility for causation or responsibility for care.

Both of our scales had been pre-tested on two populations before we used them in Blackfoot. They appear below arranged in the order of the number of positive responses received by each item.

SOCIAL DISTANCE SCALE

1. We should strongly discourage our children from marrying anyone who has been mentally ill. (*27.0 per cent of responses positive*)
2. I can imagine myself falling in love with a person who had been mentally ill. (*31.7 per cent positive*)
3. I would be willing to room with a former mental hospital patient. (*44.4 per cent positive*)
4. If I were resident owner of an apartment house I would hesitate to rent living quarters to a former mental hospital patient. (*59.8 per cent positive*)
5. If I were employed at a job I wouldn't hesitate to share my office with someone who had been mentally ill. (*70.5 per cent positive*)
6. If I owned an empty lot beside my house, I would be willing to sell it to a former mental hospital patient. (*70.6 per cent positive*)
7. I wouldn't work for anyone who had been mentally ill. (*71.3 per cent positive*)
8. I would be willing to sponsor a person who had been mentally ill for membership in my favorite club or society. (*78.3 per cent positive*)

SOCIAL RESPONSIBILITY SCALE

1. Those who live in communities from which mentally sick people come should be considered partially responsible for their breakdown. (*23.3 per cent positive*)
2. Those who live in communities from which mentally sick people come should be considered to need mental health guidance. (*37.8 per cent positive*)
3. The family and friends of a mentally sick person ought to be considered to need mental health guidance. (*44.1 per cent positive*)
4. I would feel partially responsible if a member of my family had a serious mental breakdown. (*66.4 per cent positive*)

In the first survey it was possible to use the same 4 responsibility items in analyzing the results in the control community. However, only 6 Distance Scale items were suitable. Comparisons between the two communities were thus made with a 6-item Distance Scale and a 4-item Responsibility

POSITIVE RESPONSES* TO "CORE" SCALE ITEMS—BLACKFOOT

Item	Percentage of responses positive	
	On survey	On resurvey
RESPONSIBILITY SCALE		
1. Those who live in communities from which mentally sick people come ought to be considered partially responsible for their breakdown.	23.3	28.0
2. Those who live in communities from which mentally sick people come should be considered to need mental health guidance.	37.8	35.8
3. The family and friends of a mentally sick person ought to be considered to need mental health guidance.	44.1	43.6
4. I would feel partially responsible if a member of my family had a serious mental breakdown.	66.4	62.0
DISTANCE SCALE		
1. We should strongly discourage our children from marrying anyone who has been mentally ill.	27.0	25.2
2. I can imagine myself falling in love with a person who had been mentally ill.	31.7	31.9
3. I would be willing to room with a former mental hospital patient.	44.4	45.7
4. If I owned an empty lot beside my house I would be willing to sell it to a former mental hospital patient.	70.6	70.3
5. I would be willing to sponsor a person who had been mentally ill for membership in my favorite club or society.	78.3	74.7

* Positive responses are used as scores throughout instead of Guttman scale "types." This was done because of mechanical difficulties in computing scale types. There is, of course, a high correlation between scale type and our score.

Scale, although for internal comparisons in Blackfoot itself, the full 8-item Distance Scale was used.

In the second survey the following 2 Responsibility Scale items were added and comparison between Blackfoot and Deerville was thus made with a 6-item instrument:

The people with whom a person works on his job ought to be considered partly responsible if he becomes mentally ill.

I would feel partially responsible if a person who worked for me became mentally ill.

3. *The Scale Responses Compared*

The tables in this and following sections show the relative numbers of positive responses to those "core" scale items which were considered to constitute unidimensional scales both on survey and resurvey, and can therefore be used to compare Blackfoot with Deerville both before and after the education program. The totals for various comparisons are not always the same; if score is being related, for example, to age, only those respondents who filled in their age can be used. When we made tests, we found that scores were neither higher nor lower among respondents who withheld such data.

Answers were dichotomous ("Agree" or "Disagree"), and a high score represents a high number of positive responses.

4. *Internal Comparisons of Scale Scores*

Comparisons by age and educational level for both the Distance and Responsibility scales were made on the Blackfoot questionnaires. We found upon analysis that scores on the Distance Scale varied directly with education and inversely with age, the younger, better-educated people saying that they felt able to tolerate more contact with mental illness than the older, less well educated. Responsibility scores were unaffected however, as Tables 3, 4, and 5 show. (In some tables the total is less than 540 because not all respondents

TABLE 3. Relation of Education to Scores on Distance and Responsibility Sca‖

Blackfoot—First Questionnaire

ITEMS POSITIVE		Grade school		Some high school		High school grad. or more		Tota‖
		No.	%	No.	%	No.	%	No.
A. DISTANCE SCALE								
0		8	(5.5)	14	(6.0)	3	(2.3)	25
1		10	(7.0)	12	(5.2)	5	(3.8)	27
2		16	(11.6)	15	(6.4)	7	(5.3)	38
3		26	(18.3)	29	(12.4)	6	(4.6)	61
4		24	(16.8)	22	(9.4)	26	(19.9)	72
5		23	(16.2)	41	(17.5)	24	(18.3)	88
6		17	(12.0)	49	(20.9)	26	(19.8)	92
7		14	(9.8)	26	(11.1)	15	(11.5)	55
8		4	(2.8)	26	(11.1)	19	(14.5)	49
	Total	142	(100.0)	234	(100.0)	131	(100.0)	507
B. RESPONSIBILITY SCALE								
0		26	(18.4)	45	(19.2)	19	(14.5)	90
1		46	(32.4)	78	(33.4)	42	(32.1)	166
2		34	(23.9)	53	(22.6)	29	(22.1)	116
3		25	(17.6)	43	(18.4)	28	(21.4)	96
4		11	(7.7)	15	(6.4)	13	(9.9)	39
	Total	142	(100.0)	234	(100.0)	131	(100.0)	507

A. DISTANCE SCALE	B. RESPONSIBILITY SCA‖
$\chi^2 = 43.42$	$\chi^2 = .83$
$P < .001$	$P = .98$

TABLE 4. Relation of Age to Scores on Distance and
Responsibility Scales

Blackfoot—First Questionnaire

ITEMS POSITIVE		RESPONDENTS					
		Under 40		Over 40		Total	
		No.	%	No.	%	No.	%
A. DISTANCE SCALE							
0		7	(2.9)	17	(6.0)	24	(4.6)
1		11	(4.6)	19	(6.8)	30	(5.8)
2		9	(3.8)	31	(11.0)	40	(7.7)
3		16	(6.7)	49	(17.4)	65	(12.5)
4		26	(10.8)	46	(16.4)	72	(13.8)
5		44	(18.4)	45	(16.0)	89	(17.1)
6		53	(22.2)	41	(14.6)	94	(18.1)
7		31	(13.0)	24	(8.5)	55	(10.6)
8		42	(17.6)	9	(3.2)	51	(9.8)
	Total	239	(100.0)	281	(100.0)	520	(100.0)
B. RESPONSIBILITY SCALE							
0		41	(17.2)	49	(17.4)	90	(17.3)
1		83	(34.7)	84	(29.9)	167	(32.2)
2		58	(24.3)	66	(23.5)	124	(23.8)
3		39	(16.3)	60	(21.4)	99	(19.0)
4		18	(7.5)	22	(7.8)	40	(7.7)
	Total	239	(100.0)	281	(100.0)	520	(100.0)

A. DISTANCE SCALE   B. RESPONSIBILITY SCALE
$\chi^2 = 80.59$ $\chi^2 = 2.71$
$P < .001$ $.70 > P > .50$

TABLE 5. Relation of Both Age and Education to Scores on Distance and Responsibility Scales

Blackfoot—First Questionnaire

ITEMS POSITIVE		RESPONDENTS					
		Under 40; high sch. grad. or more		Over 40; less than grade 8		Total	
		No.	%	No.	%	No.	%
A. DISTANCE SCALE							
0–1–2		5	(9.3)	25	(26.0)	30	(20.0)
3–4		7	(12.9)	41	(42.8)	48	(32.0)
5–6		21	(38.9)	20	(20.8)	41	(27.3)
7–8		21	(38.9)	10	(10.4)	31	(20.7)
	Total	54	(100.0)	96	(100.0)	150	(100.0)
B. RESPONSIBILITY SCALE							
0		7	(13.0)	16	(16.7)	23	(15.3)
1		20	(37.0)	34	(35.4)	54	(36.0)
2		12	(22.2)	28	(29.2)	40	(26.7)
3		10	(18.5)	11	(11.5)	21	(14.0)
4		5	(9.3)	7	(7.3)	12	(8.0)
	Total	54	(100.0)	96	(100.0)	150	(100.0)

A. DISTANCE SCALE
$\chi^2 = 32.69$
$P < .001$

B. RESPONSIBILITY SCALE
$\chi^2 = 1.80$
$P > .90$

gave both age and education, or, as in Table 5, not all respondents are used.)

These three tables demonstrate that we are dealing with two sets of attitudes which are not only *technically* different, as the scaling process demonstrates, but are also *socially* different, inasmuch as they appear to fit into different social nexuses. Furthermore, the variability of each scale is quite independent of the other. Even when extreme categories of respondents—such as the oldest, least educated and the youngest, best educated—are used and the respondents of medium age and education are dropped out, as they are in Table 5, the Responsibility scores fail to show any variance with the variables of age and education to which the Distance Scale is so sensitive.

A consistent finding which was totally unexpected and which complements the finding that these two attitudes arise in different social nexuses is that the Distance and Responsibility scales were entirely unrelated to each other over the whole sample population and no relationships could be found when age, education, "cause," or any other subgroups were tested. Table 6 shows this very clearly. (No other tables demonstrating this lack of relationship are reproduced; however 42 such tests were made and all but one showed random distribution. The forty-second test showed a degree of relationship which would have been expected once out of 20 times by chance alone! We conclude firmly that no relationship exists.)

Because of this persistent failure of association between scores on the Distance and Responsibility scales, certain pairs of individual items whose content appeared to be logically related were chosen for tests of concordance. The pairs listed were tested, and as Table 7 reveals, it is impossible to predict from the response to any one of each set of items what the response to the pair will be.

Apparently independence of response to the Responsibility and Distance questions is consistent right down to the individual items, and chance alone appears to govern the combinations of scores.*

The implication of this finding that the Distance and Responsibility scales are totally unrelated is a little hard to grasp. It is easy to visualize and to understand a *negative*

---

* Dr. Louis Guttman used these data in demonstrating the facet analysis at Harvard University in 1954. He concluded that our items were related in terms of their "third component"; but for the level of analysis undertaken here we can consider them unrelated.

TABLE 6. Relation of Distance and Responsibility Scores to One Another

Blackfoot—First Questionnaire

DISTANCE ITEMS POSITIVE	RESPONDENTS, BY NO. OF RESPONSIBILITY ITEMS POSITIVE										RESPONDENTS TOTAL	
	0 item		1 item		2 items		3 items		4 items			
	No.	%	No.	%	No.	%	No.	%	No.	%	No.	%
0	5	(5.2)	8	(4.7)	6	(4.8)	9	(8.6)	1	(2.4)	29	(5.4)
1	11	(11.3)	6	(3.5)	9	(7.1)	5	(4.8)	1	(2.4)	32	(5.9)
2	9	(9.4)	9	(5.3)	10	(7.9)	10	(9.5)	3	(7.3)	41	(7.6)
3	12	(12.4)	22	(12.9)	18	(14.3)	12	(11.4)	6	(14.6)	70	(13.0)
4	15	(15.5)	31	(18.1)	14	(11.1)	11	(10.5)	5	(12.2)	76	(14.1)
5	12	(12.4)	23	(13.5)	26	(20.6)	19	(18.1)	9	(22.0)	89	(16.5)
6	14	(14.4)	36	(21.0)	22	(17.5)	18	(17.1)	5	(12.2)	95	(17.5)
7	10	(10.3)	19	(11.1)	11	(8.8)	13	(12.4)	4	(9.8)	57	(10.6)
8	9	(9.3)	17	(9.9)	10	(7.9)	8	(7.6)	7	(17.1)	51	(9.4)
Total	97	(100.0)	171	(100.0)	126	(100.0)	105	(100.0)	41	(100.0)	540	(100.0)

$$\chi^2 = 29.89$$
$$P > .70$$

PAIRS OF ITEMS TESTED FOR CONCORDANCE

PAIR I

a. If I were employed at a job I wouldn't hesitate to share my office with someone who had been mentally ill. (*Distance*)

b. I would feel partially responsible if a person who worked for me became mentally ill. (*Responsibility*)

PAIR II

a. If I were employed at a job I wouldn't hesitate to share my office with someone who had been mentally ill. (*Distance*)

b. The people with whom a person works on his job ought to be considered partly responsible if he becomes mentally ill. (*Responsibility*)

PAIR III

a. I wouldn't work for anyone who had been mentally ill. (*Distance*)

b. I would feel partially responsible if a person who worked for me became mentally ill. (*Responsibility*)

PAIR IV

a. I wouldn't work for anyone who had been mentally ill. (*Distance*)

b. The person with whom a person works on his job ought to be considered partially responsible if he becomes mentally ill. (*Responsibility*)

PAIR V

a. The personal friends of a mentally ill person ought to be considered partly responsible for his breakdown. (*Responsibility*)

b. I would be willing to sponsor a person who had been mentally ill for membership in my favorite club or society. (*Distance*)

TABLE 7. Concordance between Pairs of Logically Related Items
Blackfoot—Second Questionnaire

LOGICALLY RELATED ITEMS	RESPONDENTS					
	Negative item B		Positive item B		Total	
	No.	%	No.	%	No.	%
PAIR I						
Positive item a	95	(28.8)	32	(29.6)	127	(29.0)
Negative item a	235	(71.2)	76	(70.4)	311	(71.0)
Total	330	(100.0)	108	(100.0)	438	(100.0)
PAIR II						
Positive item a	81	(24.7)	33	(29.7)	114	(26.0)
Negative item a	246	(75.2)	78	(70.3)	324	(74.0)
Total	327	(100.0)	111	(100.0)	438	(100.0)
PAIR III						
Positive item a	98	(32.6)	35	(25.5)	133	(30.4)
Negative item a	203	(67.4)	102	(74.5)	305	(69.6)
Total	301	(100.0)	137	(100.0)	438	(100.0)
PAIR IV						
Positive item a	81	(27.3)	40	(28.4)	121	(27.6)
Negative item a	216	(72.7)	101	(71.6)	317	(72.4)
Total	297	(100.0)	141	(100.0)	438	(100.0)
PAIR V						
Positive item a	105	(73.4)	226	(76.6)	331	(75.6)
Negative item a	38	(26.6)	69	(23.4)	107	(24.4)
Total	143	(100.0)	295	(100.0)	438	(100.0)

PAIR I
$\chi^2 = .02$
$.90 > P > .80$

PAIR II
$\chi^2 = .82$
$.50 > P > .30$

PAIR III
$\chi^2 = 1.87$
$.20 > P > .10$

PAIR IV
$\chi^2 = .15$
$.70 > P > .50$

PAIR V
$\chi^2 = .37$
$.70 > P > .50$

relationship in which a person claims heavy responsibility for mental illness as a problem in order to compensate for unwillingness to be close to the mentally ill or vice versa. Our situation is that it is *impossible* to predict from any person's score on one scale what they would be *most likely* to score on the other, and this is rather a difficult state of affairs to fix securely in the mind. There is a natural tendency to try to "explain" unrelatedness. Logically, there is no need to explain unrelatedness at all, but rather there is a need to explain why we are so surprised when relationship is lacking. We do not try to explain why hat size in Dallas, Texas, is unrelated to temperature in Nome, Alaska, because we never expected a relationship. However, when two sets of questions, both of which contain the term "mental illness" are unrelated we realize that we had a very strong latent belief that they would be. Some discussions of technical reasons for unrelatedness appear in Appendix II along with the consideration of the ambiguity of meaning in the Responsibility Scale, but we will present in the following paragraphs a tentative explanation of this surprising result of our analysis.

In a complicated society such as ours, there are always a number of built-in contradictions which tend to cause conflict within people. For example, in our predominantly Christian society, most of us agree that the precept "love thy neighbor" describes an ideal of behavior to which we aspire. At the same time we admire independence and initiative and we place a high value upon success, especially in competition with others. Sometimes achieving success and loving one's neighbors come into conflict. Perhaps this does not happen too often, but when it does it is very uncomfortable. However, there are ways to neutralize or prevent such conflict, and one of these is by insulation of potentially conflicting beliefs from one another. Thus we do not actually carry our religious principles into the marketplace; rather we have a slightly different set of principles or ethics to guide us there. Naturally, the two cannot be in radical conflict, but it is possible to avoid potential strife around the edges of these belief systems through insulating them from one another.

There is a possibility that, in this same way, the responses to our two scales arise from different nexuses of behavior and belief. It may be that the Distance Scale belongs to an area of conviction which for psychological security reasons is insulated from the area from which the answers to the Responsibility questions arise. It may be that the Distance Scale probes a less rational, more personal and private attitude dimension than does the other, and is therefore insulated from, and thus unrelated to, the content of the more public attitudes tapped by the Responsibility Scale.

Turning back to the questionnaires we found that in the first survey 400 Blackfoot respondents out of 540 offered an opinion regarding what they considered to be the main cause of mental illness. Although the meaning of some of the statements as they stand on the questionnaires is equivocal, the intensive interviews asked detailed questions about the cause of mental illness, and the answers were used to strengthen our interpretations of the questionnaire responses.

The following system of categories was developed for the purpose of analyzing the responses to the question, "What do you consider to be the main cause of mental illness?"

1. Failure or breakdown of the biological organism
    a. Hereditary causes and congenital causes: "mostly hereditary," "mental illness is chiefly the result of the environment, however it is persons who have inherited a mentally weak condition who crack under the strain," "hereditary mental weakness," "it runs in some families," etc.
    b. Physical illness and injury: "accidents to the head," "a lot of sickness," "poor health," etc.
    c. "Nerves" when included in a biological context: "the nerves," "nervous conditions," "bad nerves," "a growth pressing on the nerves," etc.

2. Disorders of the personality system
   a. Flaws in personality or character: "inability to adjust yourself to problems," "it's mostly caused within yourself—lack of a sound philosophy of life," "letting yourself dwell on one thing," "hatred," "jealousy."
   b. Worry, unspecified or needless: "worry," "a lot of useless worry."
   c. "Nerves" when anxiety and conflict are implied: "worry, mental strain, and grief," "worry over inability to cope with a situation."
3. Breakdown or failure in interaction systems (social system)
   a. Interpersonal and family: "family troubles," "lack of love," "lack of sympathetic understanding," "childhood environment," "not a happy home life."
   b. Community, i.e., failure of group integration; complexity of industrialized society: "no sense of security in living," "not on equal terms," "human nerves have not been able to adjust to the rigors of the machine age," "not belonging, in a social sense, in the community."
   c. Exigencies (deaths, disasters, frustrations arising in the situation): "unfortunate circumstances which pile up so that one can no longer form a satisfactory one-to-one relationship with life," "death of a loved one," "a sudden shock."
4. Breakdown of institutionalized values, or institutionalization of harmful values (culture)
   a. Religion or lack of it, i.e., sectism or lack of spiritual values: "lack of religious training as children," "too much religion," "irreligion," "complete lack of faith in God and in the future," "religious fanaticism."
   b. The "state of the world": "the pace of modern life," "this modern world," "wars and rumors of wars," "one hears and reads so much confusing propaganda that one loses faith in everything and becomes bewildered."
   c. Corrupting effect of institutionalized "excesses" such as drinking: "too much smoking and drinking and fast living," "too much talk about sex," "lack of appreciation of fun as compared to sensationalism," "too much secrecy surrounding sex."
5. Economic disruption
   a. Financial problems: "financial worry," "hard times."
   b. The effects of a low standard of living, "debts," "high cost of living," etc. (The theme here is poverty per se rather than social disintegration.)

Clearly, with unprobed paper-and-pencil responses, it is possible that many respondents' replies were misinterpreted. The decision to categorize any one answer in one way rather than another was a subjective judgment influenced considerably by the types of responses given in the intensive interviews. Although these responses may have been erroneously categorized in some cases, the results are very suggestive. A total of 172 people mentioned some biological reason as the main cause of mental illness, either alone or in combination with other causes. Two hundred and seven gave reasons which were assignable to the personality of the ill person, 133 gave disruption of the social system as a cause, 99 mentioned reasons which were relatable to culture, and 86 gave economic causes. There was a tendency for those scoring higher on both scales to give multiple causes more often than the lower-scoring people.

We then sorted respondents according to the *main* cause of mental illness given. In most cases this sorting was quite simple, as the list of causes tended to be overweighted in the direction of one or the other categories, but when two causes given were clearly alternative, the first mentioned was used. Only 10 of the 400 responses could not be assigned because the meaning was felt to be too obscure for a reasonable guess to be made at the proper category, or because the answer was clearly facetious—the respondent who said that driving on Prairie Province roads was the main cause of mental illness was judged to be making a traditional joke rather than commenting seriously upon the economic deprivation of the Province. A comparison of the mean scores is given in Table 8.

The difference between the mean scores of the Distance Scale is not quite significant and so does not convince us that there is an over-all difference, although the difference between the scores made by those giving biological causes and all others is very striking, as Table 8 shows. The table dem-

TABLE 8. Mean Scores, Distance and Responsibility Scales,
by Causes of Mental Illness

Blackfoot—First Questionnaire

| SCALE | MEAN SCORES, BY CAUSES OF MENTAL ILLNESS CITED | | | | |
	Social system	Economic	Culture	Personality	Biological
Distance	5.18	5.02	4.90	4.78	4.05
Responsibility	2.00	2.13	1.45	1.61	1.39

onstrates, however, a clear-cut relationship between the opinion that people hold as to the causes of mental illness and their feeling of responsibility for mental illness.

It is perhaps not surprising that those who see the causes of mental illness residing in the economic or social system also consider themselves responsible for it, while those who see the cause as biological disclaim responsibility. Especially is this likely to be true in a Province with a long history of radicalism of the sort which heavily emphasizes social welfare. Tentatively, we might predict that people will feel more responsibility for a problem if they see the causes—or cures—of that problem amenable to manipulation at the large-group level, that is, through legislation, reform, and so on, than if the causes are essentially inside people. This hypothesis accounts for part of the ordering of causes by score which we have seen, and it deserves empirical testing.

Here, as in all subgroups of the original survey, Distance and Responsibility Scale scores are independent of one another; the respondents show the same *random association* between the two scores when sorted by cause of mental illness as they had when sorted by age and education; the insulation appears perfect.

To summarize, the community, judging from our sample, is one in which social distance from those who have been mentally ill is affected directly by the age and inversely by the education of the respondents, whereas social responsibility, unaffected by these variables, is influenced by what the respondent sees as the cause of mental illness. The highest-scoring group on the Responsibility Scale were those people who saw economic causes as most critical, followed by those who blamed defects in the social system. Those who assigned the cause to breakdown in personality followed, while those seeing flaws in the individual's or society's moral values or in biological faults were the least willing to assume responsibility for mental illness.

Having developed an over-all picture of the kinds of responses made by Blackfoot people to our questioning, we turned to the sample of questionnaires collected in Deerville, a town chosen, as we have described, for its similarity to the experimental community.

When we analyzed the control community, where 107 questionnaires were administered to a random sample of the population, we found no difference between it and Blackfoot on Responsibility Scale scores. On the Distance Scale the Blackfoot population came close to scoring higher than the Deerville sample. We cannot, with this amount of difference, eliminate the possibility that it had occurred by chance alone (Table 9).

The differences in Distance Scale scores may be a result of a selection factor in Blackfoot, because those who were interested enough to return the questionnaire may have tended to get higher scores; the Deerville sample was random. In the light of the fact that score on the Distance Scale seems to vary quite readily with a number of factors, it is quite possible that willingness to return the questionnaire acted as another such variable as age and education.

We concluded that our experimental community did not differ very much from our control community; in both Blackfoot and Deerville the younger, better-educated people said they were more willing to associate with those who had been

TABLE 9. Comparison of Blackfoot and Deerville—
First Questionnaire

ITEMS POSITIVE		RESPONDENTS					
		Blackfoot		Deerville		Total	
		No.	%	No.	%	No.	%
A. DISTANCE SCALE							
0–1		91	(16.9)	32	(29.9)	123	(19.0)
2		88	(16.3)	18	(16.8)	106	(16.4)
3		114	(21.1)	16	(15.0)	130	(20.1)
4		116	(21.5)	22	(20.6)	138	(21.3)
5		71	(13.2)	11	(10.2)	82	(12.7)
6		60	(11.0)	8	(7.5)	69	(10.5)
	Total	540	(100.0)	107	(100.0)	647	(100.0)
B. RESPONSIBILITY SCALE							
0		97	(18.0)	12	(11.2)	109	(16.8)
1		171	(31.7)	31	(29.0)	202	(31.2)
2		126	(23.3)	26	(24.3)	152	(23.5)
3		105	(19.4)	27	(25.2)	132	(20.4)
4		41	(7.6)	11	(10.3)	52	(8.1)
	Total	540	(100.0)	107	(100.0)	647	(100.0)

A. DISTANCE SCALE	B. RESPONSIBILITY SCALE
$\chi^2 = 11.19$	$\chi^2 = 4.93$
$.05 > P > .02$	$.30 > P > .20$

mentally ill than the older, less well educated, and the perceived cause of mental illness strongly influenced the declared willingness of the citizens to take some order of responsibility for mental illness. In short, Deerville was, as we had expected, little different from Blackfoot.

5. Before-After Comparison of Scale Scores

Analyses of scale scores on the first and second questionnaires in both experimental and the control community were

made. The scale scores in both were unchanged. No education had been attempted in the control community, and this
community had had only the stimulation which was available
to the general public. At this time in Canada there was a
quite considerable interest in mental health topics. The Canadian Broadcasting Corporation, for example, produced
regular weekly programs about mental health.

Tables 10 and 11 show the before-after picture of the

TABLE 10. Comparison in Deerville—First and Second Questionnaires

ITEMS POSITIVE		RESPONDENTS					
		First quest.		Second quest.		Total	
		No.	%	No.	%	No.	%
A. DISTANCE SCALE							
0		9	(8.4)	10	(9.4)	19	(8.9)
1		23	(21.5)	16	(14.9)	39	(18.2)
2		18	(16.8)	13	(12.2)	31	(14.5)
3		16	(14.9)	23	(21.5)	39	(18.2)
4		22	(20.6)	24	(22.4)	46	(21.5)
5		11	(10.3)	15	(14.0)	26	(12.2)
6		8	(7.5)	6	(5.6)	14	(6.5)
	Total	107	(100.0)	107	(100.0)	214	(100.0)
B. RESPONSIBILITY SCALE							
0		12	(11.2)	19	(17.8)	31	(14.5)
1		31	(29.0)	20	(18.7)	51	(23.8)
2		26	(24.3)	24	(22.4)	50	(23.4)
3		27	(25.2)	21	(19.6)	48	(22.4)
4		11	(10.3)	23	(21.5)	34	(15.9)
	Total	107	(100.0)	107	(100.0)	214	(100.0)

A. DISTANCE SCALE $\chi^2 = 4.36$ $.70 > P > .50$

B. RESPONSIBILITY SCALE $\chi^2 = 9.02$ $.10 > P > .05$

TABLE 11. Comparison in Blackfoot—First and Second Questionnaires

ITEMS POSITIVE		First quest. No.	First quest. %	Second quest. No.	Second quest. %	Total No.	Total %
A. DISTANCE SCALE							
0–1		91	(16.9)	79	(18.0)	170	(17.4)
2		88	(16.3)	51	(11.6)	139	(14.2)
3		114	(21.1)	91	(20.8)	205	(21.0)
4		116	(21.5)	94	(21.5)	210	(21.5)
5		71	(13.1)	68	(15.5)	139	(14.2)
6		60	(11.1)	55	(12.6)	115	
	Total	540	(100.0)	438	(100.0)	978	
B. RESPONSIBILITY SCALE							
0		97	(18.0)	109	(24.9)	206	(21.1)
1		171	(31.7)	102	(23.3)	273	(27.9)
2		126	(23.3)	96	(21.9)	222	(22.7)
3		105	(19.4)	87	(19.9)	192	(19.6)
4		41	(7.6)	44	(10.0)	85	(8.7)
	Total	540	(100.0)	438	(100.0)	978	(100.0)
C. RESPONSIBILITY SCALE WITH SCORES COMBINED TO CONCEAL CHANGE IN VARIANCE							
0–1–2		394	(73.0)	307	(70.1)	701	(71.7)
3–4		146	(27.0)	131	(29.1)	277	(28.3)
	Total	540	(100.0)	438	(100.0)	978	(100.0)

A. DISTANCE SCALE
$\chi^2 = 5.28$
$.50 > P > .30$

B. RESPONSIBILITY SCALE
$\chi^2 = 13.49$
$P < .01$

C. RESPONSIBILITY SCALE WITH SCORES COMBINED TO CONCEAL CHANGE IN VARIANCE
$\chi^2 = .85$
$.50 > P > .30$

Responsibility Scale in Deerville and in Blackfoot. It can be seen that there is some difference in distribution, but this does not reach significance and the mean score is unchanged.

Upon calculating variations in score by age and education, we found that in Blackfoot the Distance Scale scores on the second questionnaire still varied with education as they had before (see Table 12).

Feeling that the study group had experienced the greatest impact of the program, we tested the difference in score on both scales between its members and the entire higher education group—most of the study group were also of this educational class—and found no difference. The higher score, which is associated with higher education on the Distance Scale, is accounted for, to our surprise, by the difference between the "grade school only" group and all others; there is *no difference* between those with "some high school" and those with "high school graduation or more." Apparently the decision to go to high school is critically related to attitudes to mental illness, in this population.

Upon resurvey, the difference in Distance Scale score between the "under forty" and "over forty" age groups only approached significance, a much smaller difference than was found at the time of the first survey (Table 13).

The Responsibility Scale score was unaffected by age or education at the time of the original survey, and while remaining unaffected by age upon resurvey, tended on the second time to vary with educational level (Table 14).*

* At this point it might be well to point out, however, that this difference in Responsibility score falls between the 5-per-cent and the 2-per-cent levels of significance. The method of testing differences, being based upon the binominal distribution, undoubtedly overestimates the extent of all of these differences, leaving the reality of this particular one very much in doubt. Furthermore, among such a large number of tests (several hundred were performed), one would, by normal probability, expect a certain number of differences of this magnitude to occur by chance alone. It is for the reasons mentioned above that probabilities exceeding the 2-per-cent level are not regarded as significant in this study.

TABLE 12. Variation in Distance Scale Score with Education

Blackfoot—First and Second Questionnaires

ITEMS POSITIVE	RESPONDENTS: FIRST QUESTIONNAIRE						RESPONDENTS: SECOND QUESTIONNAIRE					
	Grade school only		Some high school		High school grad. or more		Grade school only		Some high school		High school grad. or more	
	No.	%	No.	%	No.	%	No.	%	No.	%	No.	%
0–1	28	(19.7)	36	(15.4)	11	(8.4)	28	(21.9)	26	(14.2)	10	(12.3)
2	32	(22.5)	37	(15.8)	16	(12.2)	20	(15.6)	14	(7.7)	12	(14.8)
3	36	(25.3)	36	(15.4)	37	(28.2)	28	(21.9)	33	(18.0)	18	(22.3)
4	23	(16.3)	61	(26.1)	28	(21.4)	29	(22.7)	43	(23.5)	14	(17.3)
5	18	(12.7)	34	(14.5)	18	(13.7)	14	(10.9)	35	(19.1)	14	(17.3)
6*	5	(3.5)	30	(12.8)	21	(16.1)	9	(7.0)	32	(17.5)	13	(16.0)
Total	142	(100.0)	234	(100.0)	131	(100.0)	128	(100.0)	183	(100.0)	81	(100.0)

FIRST QUEST.
$\chi^2 = 43.42$
$P < .001$
Total: 507

SECOND QUEST.
$\chi^2 = 20.01$
$P < .01$
Total: 392†

* Six scale items are used for comparison because only 6 distance items were scalable in Blackfoot and Deerville on both the first and second questionnaires.
† Not all respondents gave their education.

TABLE 13. Variation in Distance Scale Score with Age

Blackfoot—First and Second Questionnaires

ITEMS POSITIVE	RESPONDENTS: FIRST QUESTIONNAIRE						RESPONDENTS: SECOND QUESTIONNAIRE					
	Under 40		Over 40		Total		Under 40		Over 40		Total	
	No.	%	No.	%	No.	%	No.	%	No.	%	No.	%
0	11	(4.6)	30	(10.7)	41	(7.9)	6	(3.2)	15	(6.7)	21	(5.1)
1	11	(4.6)	27	(9.6)	38	(7.3)	20	(10.7)	28	(12.4)	48	(11.7)
2	26	(10.9)	59	(20.0)	85	(16.4)	20	(10.7)	30	(13.3)	50	(12.1)
3	44	(18.4)	69	(24.5)	113	(21.7)	31	(16.6)	52	(23.2)	83	(20.1)
4	61	(25.5)	52	(18.5)	113	(21.7)	44	(23.5)	47	(20.9)	91	(22.1)
5	37	(15.5)	34	(12.1)	71	(13.7)	34	(18.2)	32	(14.2)	66	(16.0)
6	49	(20.5)	10	(3.6)	59	(11.3)	32	(17.1)	21	(9.3)	53	(12.9)
Total	239	(100.0)	281	(100.0)	520	(100.0)	187	(100.0)	225	(100.0)	412	(100.0)

FIRST QUEST.
$\chi^2 = 80.59$
$P < .001$

SECOND QUEST.
$\chi^2 = 11.54$
$.10 > P > .05$

TABLE 14. Variation of Score on Responsibility Scale with Education
Blackfoot—Second Questionnaire

		RESPONDENTS							
		Grade school education		Some high school		High school grad. or more		Total	
MS		No.	%	No.	%	No.	%	No.	%
IVE									
		33	(25.8)	47	(25.7)	13	(16.1)	93	(23.7)
		24	(18.8)	24	(13.0)	14	(17.3)	62	(15.8)
		22	(17.2)	37	(20.2)	10	(12.3)	69	(17.6)
		24	(18.8)	29	(15.9)	15	(18.5)	68	(17.4)
		14	(10.9)	25	(13.7)	7	(8.6)	46	(11.7)
		6	(4.7)	11	(6.0)	11	(13.6)	28	(7.2)
		5	(3.8)	10	(5.5)	11	(13.6)	26	(6.6)
	Total	128	(100.0)	183	(100.0)	81	(100.0)	392	(100.0)

$$\chi^2 = 22.37$$
$$.05 > P > .02$$

TABLE 15. Comparison of Mean Scores, Distance and Responsibility Scales
Blackfoot and Deerville—First and Second Questionnaires

	RESPONSIBILITY SCALE						DISTANCE SCALE					
	First quest.			Second quest.			First quest.			Second quest.		
	Mean	P.E.	S.D.	Mean	P.E.	S.D.	Mean	P.E.	S.D.	Mean	P.E.	S.D.
oot	1.67	.05	1.19	1.67	.06	1.31	3.21	.09	2.13	3.17	.14	2.25
lle	1.90	.11	1.09	2.08	.13	1.32	2.79	.17	1.74	2.97	.16	1.68

The mean score on the Responsibility Scale remained unchanged at the time of the resurvey, as we have noted above and as Table 15 shows.

In the resurvey two new variables, rental area and a new "value variable"* were introduced. The latter consisted in responses to the questions: "What kind of man is really respected in this community?" "What kind of woman is really respected?" "What kind of child is really liked?" A total of 242 people wrote replies to these questions.

It is assumed in the succeeding analysis that the respondents gave their own preferences in answering this question unless they specifically distinguished between themselves and the rest of the community. The oral responses of a small group of male nurses, well known to us, to this question strengthen our belief that this is a safe assumption. These men tended to describe themselves when we asked them this question, and continued to do so when their responses were probed.

Descriptions of the most respected man appeared to us to fall into three major groups. The first centered on a constellation of qualities containing some or all of the following descriptive terms: "honest," "clean-living," "moral," "Christian," "temperate," "kind," "hard-working," "a good provider," "conscientious," and "helpful." This description will be referred to hereafter as a *Type I Man*. The *Type II Man* was described by some or all of the following terms: "congenial," "good mixer," "good family man," "good business man" or "successful business man," "active in community affairs," "concerned with the community welfare," "a club worker," and "executive member of organizations." A total of 125 descriptions of the kind of man respected in Blackfoot were classed as Type I and 59 as Type II.

Type III descriptions were few in number but clearly dis-

---

* We are greatly indebted to Professor Jules Henry of Washington University for suggesting the inclusion of a variable of this type.

tinguished by their cynicism. The responses displayed dissatisfaction or disillusionment with the community and its values by descriptions such as "the one who has the most money" or "the one who gets away with everything short of murder." There were 18 making such responses, and they distinguished clearly between themselves and the remainder of the community, dissociating themselves from the town and its values. Neither of the other groups did this, appearing to be identified with the society in which they lived.

A residual group of 40 responses was divided almost equally among three small classes. One group specifically named certain community prestige figures such as "our doctor" or "our minister" or gave these people's names. A small number described "men of good will," a concept which did not have the "puritan virtue" quality of Type I or the "joiner" quality of Type II. Finally a small number of responses could not be interpreted meaningfully at all and therefore were not classified.

Following the classification of the men, we made an independent analysis of the descriptions of the women. The children were then analyzed independently of the men and the women, and finally all three were tested for their association with one another. All three were coded independently by both of us.

The women were not quite so easy to classify as the men, but we were able to distinguish three categories without difficulty. A total of 117 women were described in some combination of the terms, "honest," "straightforward," "sincere," "Christian," "God-fearing," "temperate," "good housekeepers," "good homemaker," "kind to neighbors," "charitable," "helpful," and—very occasionally—"good mother." These we called *Type I Women* and predicted that they would be associated with Type I men; that is that the respondents who admired the male virtues classified as Type I would also admire the female virtues classified as Type I, as they both appeared to center on the puritan Christian tradition.

We distinguished a second group of 39 descriptions of admired women which included the virtue "active in community affairs." Generally this phrase occurred with one or more of "good homemaker," "good housekeeper," "good mother," and "good wife." These were *Type II Women,* and because of the orientation to community affairs we predicted that they would be admired by those who admired Type II men.

Seventeen respondents wrote cynical remarks regarding the type of women respected in the town, and the balance was composed of groups of less than 10 each as follows:

(a) Women described primarily in terms of being good wives and mothers without mention of any other virtues.

(b) Specific prestige figures, as with the men.

(c) Unclassifiable responses.

(d) A few scattered combinations of these minor categories.

Opinion about desirable traits in children was close to unanimous. Three hundred and seventeen respondents (*Type I*) emphasized virtues of self-control almost exclusively, saying that the children best liked in the community were "clean," "neat," "well-behaved," "courteous," "obedient," "respectful." Another 53 added "cheerful," "happy," or "agreeable" to the above list of qualities, usually at the end; these we called *Type II.* A group of 26 people included in their description children who cooperated well in playing with other children, but only 16 people gave answers which we could call "child-oriented." These included such responses as, "All children should be liked" and "Children are children and all are nice if you take the trouble to get to know them." Groups of less than 10 each gave cynical responses (*Type III*) such as "the children of the people with the most money," responses emphasizing success at school without any accompanying characteristic, or responses of such obscure meaning as to be unclassifiable.

Testing for concordance, we found that the Type I Man was admired most often by those who also admired the Type I Woman and the Type I Child. In the same way the Type II descriptions tended to fall together and so did the Type III responses. All of these tendencies were highly significant statistically. Table 16 shows in summary form this tendency toward "clumping" which makes us believe that we have tapped a genuine preference system.

Table 17 shows the result of testing value type against rental area, the second new variable used in the resurvey, and against education and age. Here we see that the Type II group lives in the medium and high rental areas more often than do the others, although the difference is not striking and might be a chance one. They are however, markedly younger and better educated than the others. In short, there seems to be a fairly genuine "type," the young, civic-minded,

TABLE 16. Concordance between Male, Female, and Child
Value Preferences

Blackfoot—Second Questionnaire

PREFERRED CHILD	TYPE I MALES: PREFERRED FEMALE		TYPE II MALES: PREFERRED FEMALE		TYPE III MALES: PREFERRED FEMALE	
	Same type	Different type	Same type	Different type	Same type	Different type
Same type	84	10	18	8	9	2
Different type	17	15	12	8	3	4

$$\chi^2 = 32.83$$
$$P < .001$$

TABLE 17. Relation of Type II and Other Respondents to Rental
Area, Education, and Age

Blackfoot—Second Questionnaire

	TYPE II MALES*		ALL OTHERS		TOTAL	
	No.	%	No.	%	No.	%
A. RENTAL AREA						
High and medium rent	36	(63.2)	79	(45.1)	115	(49.6)
Low rent	21	(36.8)	96	(54.9)	117	(50.4)
Total	57	(100.0)	175	(100.0)	232	(100.0)
B. EDUCATION						
High school grad. or more	18	(32.1)	29	(16.9)	47	(20.6)
Some high school	32	(57.1)	73	(42.4)	105	(46.1)
Grade school only	6	(10.7)	70	(40.7)	76	(33.3)
Total	56	(100.0)	172	(100.0)	228	(100.0)
C. AGE						
Over 40 years	19	(36.5)	105	(59.7)	124	(54.4)
Under 40 years	33	(63.5)	71	(40.3)	104	(45.6)
Total	52	(100.0)	176	(100.0)	228	(100.0)

A. RENTAL AREA	B. EDUCATION	C. AGE
$\chi^2 = 4.88$	$\chi^2 = 18.16$	$\chi^2 = 10.37$
$.05 > P > .02$	$P < .01$	$P < .001$

* Males were used as an index in this analysis.

well-educated man who takes an active part in community
affairs, or who at least is identified with those who do.*

Type I respondents, on the other hand, are less well edu-

* In all of these tests the category assigned to the male is used as the index
to the respondents. If they admire the Type II virtues in men, it is assumed,
as the concordance is so high, that they will also admire the Type II virtues
in women and children.

cated and are older than the others (Table 18). They admire the "puritan" virtues, and their area of interest and involvement seems narrower than that of the Type II's. Except for the age difference, we might almost be dealing with a socioeconomic class variable[41]; that is, the Type I's may have a working class value orientation while the Type II's are middle class in their approach to life.

When we started to analyze the scores, we had two main types of respondents to consider. The larger of the two groups, Type I, expressed values which may be thought of as focused on man's relationship to God, while the smaller group, Type II, had values which seemed focused on man's relationship to man. We found that the Type II respondents

TABLE 18. Relation of Type I Respondents to Education and Age

Blackfoot—Second Questionnaire

		TYPE I MALES		ALL OTHERS		TOTAL	
		No.	%	No.	%	No.	%
A. EDUCATION							
High school grad. or more		19	(16.4)	28	(25.0)	47	(20.6)
Some high school		45	(38.8)	60	(53.6)	105	(46.1)
Grade school only		52	(44.8)	24	(21.4)	76	(33.3)
	Total	116	(100.0)	112	(100.0)	228	(100.0)
B. AGE							
Over 40 years		70	(70.0)	54	(42.2)	124	(54.4)
Under 40 years		30	(30.0)	74	(57.8)	104	(45.6)
	Total	100	(100.0)	128	(100.0)	228	(100.0)

A. EDUCATION   B. AGE

$\chi^2 = 14.12$ $\chi^2 = 22.61$

$P < .001$ $P < .001$

had higher scores on the Responsibility Scale than had either the Type I's or the residual group—that is, Type III and those unclassifiable. On the Distance Scale the Type I respondents scored lower and the Type II scored the same as the remainder of the population (Table 19). The Type III or cynical group did not vary from any subgroup in score on either scale.

TABLE 19. Relation of Value Types I and II to Scores

Blackfoot—Second Questionnaire

ITEMS POSITIVE	TYPE I MALES		TYPE II MALES		ALL OTHERS		TOTAL
	No.	%	No.	%	No.	%	No.
A. RESPONSIBILITY							
0	32	(25.6)	5	(8.5)	16	(27.5)	53
1	13	(10.4)	10	(16.9)	11	(19.0)	34
2	29	(23.2)	9	(15.3)	10	(17.2)	48
3	24	(19.2)	10	(16.9)	7	(12.1)	41
4	13	(10.4)	10	(16.9)	9	(15.5)	32
5	8	(6.4)	8	(13.6)	1	(1.7)	17
6	6	(4.8)	7	(11.9)	4	(6.9)	17
Total	125	(100.0)	59	(100.0)	58	(100.0)	242
Mean score	2.17		3.05		2.01		2.35
B. DISTANCE							
0–1	23	(18.4)	5	(8.5)	13	(22.4)	41
2	19	(15.2)	6	(10.2)	4	(6.9)	29
3	28	(22.4)	14	(23.7)	4	(6.9)	46
4	28	(22.4)	13	(22.0)	10	(17.2)	51
5	14	(11.2)	14	(23.7)	12	(20.7)	40
6	13	(10.4)	7	(11.9)	15	(25.9)	35
Total	125	(100.0)	59	(100.0)	58	(100.0)	242
Mean score	3.14		3.75		3.72		3.43

A. RESPONSIBILITY	B. DISTANCE
$\chi^2 = 22.27$	$\chi^2 = 24.30$
$P = <.001$	$P = <.001$

When it is remembered that the Responsibility Scale scores varied in the first survey with nothing but the stated main causes of mental illness, and that those who saw the causes as being defects in the economic and social systems were the high-scoring people, it is not surprising, in retrospect, to find that those who value community participation and hence accept responsibility for manipulating the economic and social system also score higher on the Responsibility Scale. Although we do not know for certain whether the people who ascribe the main cause of mental illness to defects in the social and economic system are the same as those who admire men who accept community responsibility, it seems extremely likely because the numbers in each group are of the same order of magnitude and both groups have a superior education.

A tendency toward more high and low scores and fewer medium scores on the resurvey was marked in the higher education groups (Table 20). This trend did not occur among respondents who had less than a high school education. This finding fits well with our observation that we were making far more contact with the more highly educated people in the town, and it is also coordinate with Kingsley Davis's belief that the mental health movement is the carrier of the values of the middle class and that thus its members have difficulty communicating with members of the working class. Our face-to-face contacts were largely with middle-class people. The example described earlier of our contact with the school teacher is a good one. It will be recalled, too, that as well as spontaneous friendliness, the more highly educated people displayed spontaneous outbursts of hostility.

There is no doubt in our minds that this polarizing shift in attitude was caused by our program of activity. We are not in a position to be certain which aspects of it were responsible—as we have said before, it would have taken an entirely different kind of study to evaluate specific program items—nor are we in a position to know precisely who

TABLE 20. Shift in Responsibility Scale Scores, by Education
Blackfoot—First and Second Questionnaires

ITEMS		RESPONDENTS					
		First quest.		Second quest.		Total	
POSITIVE		No.	%	No.	%	No.	%
A. GRADE SCHOOL							
0		26	(18.3)	35	(27.3)	61	(22.6)
1		46	(32.4)	34	(26.6)	80	(29.6)
2		34	(23.9)	24	(18.8)	58	(21.5)
3		25	(17.6)	25	(19.5)	50	(18.5)
4		11	(7.8)	10	(7.8)	21	(7.8)
	Total	142	(100.0)	128	(100.0)	270	(100.0)
B. HIGH SCHOOL AND MORE							
0		63	(17.3)	63	(23.9)	126	(20.0)
1		121	(33.2)	52	(19.7)	173	(27.5)
2		82	(22.5)	63	(23.9)	145	(23.1)
3		71	(19.4)	54	(20.4)	125	(19.9)
4		28	(7.6)	32	(12.1)	60	(9.5)
	Total	365	(100.0)	264	(100.0)	629	(100.0)

A. GRADE SCHOOL	B. HIGH SCHOOL AND MORE
$\chi^2 = 4.18$	$\chi^2 = 16.80$
$.50 > P > .30$	$P < .01$

shifted their attitudes toward the low scores and who toward the high, but at this time common sense would certainly suggest that those to whom the educational team were naturally congenial might be the ones to show scores which were higher after the program than before it. Unfortunately, this common-sense explanation does not in any way tell us why the scores of the Responsibility Scale should swing to the high and low poles while those of the Distance Scale did not, and thus it is at best a partial explanation.

6. *Summary*

To sum up, in Blackfoot after the conclusion of the education program the average score on our two Guttman scales had not changed. We interpret this to mean that the average person in Blackfoot was neither willing to get closer to a mentally ill person nor willing to take any more responsibility for the problem of mental illness than he had been before the program.

Social distance from the mentally ill remained, at the conclusion of the project, partly a function of education. However the age of the respondent, which accounted for some of the variance in score on the Distance Scale when the program started, was no longer related to score at its conclusion.

The new "value variable," a classification of respondents according to the type of citizen which they say they value most highly, yielded interesting relationships with the other variables as well as with scores. The younger, better-educated respondents who live in medium and high rental areas and who value participation in community affairs and service to the community are more likely to get high scores on the Responsibility Scale than are the rest of the population. On the other hand, the older, less well-educated people who value the more puritanical virtues of personal excellence tend to have lower scores on both scales. They appear to desire less social interaction with the mentally ill and less responsibility for this social problem.

The experimental community did not show any move in score which distinguished it from the control community, although one section of the Blackfoot population—the most highly educated—did, after the project, have a more polarized opinion regarding responsibility for mental illness. This polarization is shown in the occurrence of more high and low scores on the Responsibility Scale with an unchanged average.

Generally, we conclude that the six-month educational program, in its all-out attempt to improve attitudes toward mental illness, produced virtually no change in the general orientation of the population either toward the social problem of mental illness or toward the mentally ill themselves. We must now set about forming some kind of coherent explanation of this fact which may prove helpful to those who spend so much energy every year in trying to improve the attitudes of communities toward those who have been mentally ill.

Part III

The Theoretical Analysis

A Speculative Review
of Some Aspects
of the Educational Program

It was clear that we had failed in our attempt to change the orientation of the Blackfoot citizens toward mental illness, and so we turned back to the educational program, and specifically to the postulates underlying its content, in an effort to find out why this was so.

1. *Analysis of the Assumptions*

First we re-examined the three working principles outlined in Chapter III, around which the program was organized, and decided that they were naively conceived. It will be recalled that we had assumed that most lay people recognize a narrower spectrum of normal behavior than do professionals, that people do not realize that the border line between "normal" and "abnormal" states is at best vague, and that the "causes" of behavior are obscure to lay people, if indeed they recognize at all that behavior has relevant antecedent elements in the environment. In an effort to understand whether these assumptions were indeed related to our failure, we turned to a consideration of some of the content of our intensive interview schedule. (A description of the sample of people whom we interviewed appears, together with the interview schedule, in Appendix II.)

First we considered the assumption that lay people see a narrower range of normal behavior than do professionals. Turning to the interviews, we find that Blackfoot residents seem to perceive a much broader range than do the mental health workers who were trying to teach them to be more tolerant of abnormality!

Only one example of this acceptance of a wide variety of behavior will be spelled out here in detail; it is the responses of the Blackfoot respondents to seven case histories which, in the course of the interviews, were read to them. They were asked whether "anything is wrong" with the person described, whether he is "mentally ill," and whether or not the condition is serious. They were also asked questions about the cause of the behavior described in the histories.

The first case, that of a fairly clear-cut paranoid schizophrenic, reads:

Now I'd like to describe a certain kind of person and ask you a few questions about him. . . . I'm thinking of a man . . . let's call him Frank Jones . . . who is very suspicious, he doesn't trust anybody, and he's sure that everybody is against him. Sometimes he thinks that people he sees on the street are talking about him or following him around. A couple of times now he has beaten up men who didn't even know him, because he thought that they were plotting against him. The other night, he began to curse his wife terribly; then he hit her and threatened to kill her, because, he said, she was working against him too, just like everyone else.

Ninety-one per cent of our respondents thought there was something wrong with this man while 9 per cent declared there was nothing wrong. In answering the question, "What do you think makes him act this way?" people had a tendency to attribute his behavior to specific past experiences; usually this involved betrayal or ill-treatment either in childhood or more recently. They said that such experiences constituted a logical justification for a persecution feeling. There appears in the responses an effort to deny the irrationality of this behavior and to make it predictable in the light of the past. Although most respondents considered these paranoid feelings logical in the light of specific past experience such as neglect and unhappiness in childhood, a small minority felt that he had a kind of inborn "mean disposition."

Thirty-one per cent of those asked called this man "not mentally ill," while 69 per cent of respondents considered him mentally ill, giving reasons divided between his violence— one earmark of mental illness—and his delusions. One respondent said, "Anyone who believes things which aren't true is crazy." Forty-five per cent of respondents considered this a serious illness because "he might injure someone" or "get worse if not treated." A substantial minority of 24 per cent, however, agreed that his condition was mental illness, but described it as not serious and believed that it could be very easily treated either by friends who would "snap him out of it" or by a family doctor. A very few of the respondents (5 per cent) considered this normal behavior for a certain bad-tempered minority of the population ("Some people are just ornery"), and a handful thought that a physical illness or a "run-down condition" was troubling Frank Jones. Only 4 per cent said that they did not know what was wrong.

The second case describes a young girl, probably suffering from simple schizophrenia:

Now here's a young woman in her twenties; let's call her Betty Smith. . . . She has never had a job, and she doesn't seem to want to go out and look for one. She is a very quiet girl; she doesn't talk much to anyone . . . even in her own family, and she acts like she is afraid of people, especially young men her own age. She won't go out with anyone, and whenever someone comes to visit her family, she stays in her own room until they leave. She just stays by herself and daydreams all the time, and shows no interest in anything or anybody.

Seventy per cent of our respondents told us that there was "something wrong" with Betty Smith and blamed her behavior on her upbringing. Most of them thought that her parents had "repressed" her by not allowing her to have friends and companions, or by not allowing her to go into society, or perhaps by sending her to her room when guests were in the home. A few suggested a bodily deformity and a scattering thought her mentally defective. A very small number seized upon the fear of "young men of her own age" and elaborated stories of assault and rape to account for her behavior—these few respondents tended to see the effects of unwise sexual indulgence everywhere. Thirty per cent of the people who heard Betty Smith's story said that there was nothing wrong with her at all.

Sixty-four per cent denied that she was mentally ill, for after all she is harmless and there is an easy cure for her condition—it only requires understanding and sympathetic guidance to bring her around. Here our respondents reserve the concept "mental illness" for those conditions which are not curable. Indeed, when examples were used a great many more respondents *referred to mental illness as if it were incurable* than had verbalized this notion in abstract terms earlier in the same interview.*

Most respondents did not consider her condition serious, except a minority of 15 per cent. This minority considered Betty Smith to be ill because "her life is being wasted" and "she will never find happiness that way." Their definition of

* The material elicited in other parts of the interview is not analyzed here. It is doubtful whether it differs more than a slight amount from the American responses which Dr. Star will analyze exhaustively in her forthcoming volume.

ill-health hinged upon a concept of self-fulfillment which was quite lacking in the other responses, and appeared to be rooted in an unformulated standard of "mental health." Most respondents stated spontaneously that she was not mentally ill and that the condition was not serious. Only 5 per cent did not know what was wrong with this girl.

The third history, that of George Brown, a depressed man, follows:

Here's another kind of man; we can call him George Brown. He has a good job and is doing pretty well at it. Most of the time he gets along all right with people, but he is always very touchy and he always loses his temper quickly if things aren't going his way, or if people find fault with him. He worries a lot about little things, and he seems to be moody and unhappy all the time. Everything is going along all right for him, but he can't sleep nights, brooding about the past and worrying about things that *might* go wrong.

The question, "Is there anything wrong with this man?" drew 55 per cent "Something wrong," 39 per cent "Nothing wrong," and 6 per cent "Don't know." When asked, "What makes him act this way?" half of the people replied that he must have been spoiled as a child or handled in such a way as to make him "mean and nervous." Most of the respondents interpreted this handling as overindulgence. Those who thought nothing was wrong said that he was "just a worrying type," no matter what they thought was causing the worry. In other words, regardless of the type of situation causing worry, the worry is considered to be a *normal* and *proper* reaction to that situation; in brief, a "worrying type" is one of an implicit set of "normal types." Notice that this differs from Blackfoot's reaction to the description of a paranoid; in his case the extreme situation conditioned him in such a way that he acted "abnormally" even though logically. In the paranoid's case one might almost conclude it was "normal" to be "mentally ill," but in George Brown's case anxiety and depression are defined as part of the normal and acceptable range of human behavior.

Quite a substantial number of people made such remarks as "if anything is wrong with George Brown, then most of the people in this world have something wrong with them."

This case history describes, as it is undoubtedly meant to, a clinically disturbed man, and it is most interesting that 74 per cent of the respondents described him as not mentally ill. Most of the 20 per cent who thought him ill appeared to use as a frame of reference some ideal construct of "mental health."

The next case is that of an alcoholic.

How about Bill Williams? He never seems to be able to hold a job very long because he drinks so much. Whenever he has money in his pocket, he goes on a spree; he stays out till all hours drinking, and never seems to care what happens to his wife and children. Sometimes he feels very bad about the way he treats his family; he begs his wife to forgive him and promises to stop drinking, but he always goes off again.

Sixty per cent told us that there was something wrong, although a large minority (32 per cent) said, "There's nothing wrong with him, it's just the booze" or something of the sort. Of those who said, "Something wrong," almost all declared him to be weak-willed and lacking in character, with a few considering alcoholism a physical disease. There was general agreement—75 per cent—that he was not mentally ill, although almost 90 per cent thought his drinking was a serious problem. A number of people mentioned spontaneously the prevalence of "this sort of thing," evidently considering any sort of drinking to be alcoholism. The seriousness of the condition seemed to be determined, in the minds of our respondents, by the effect of his drinking upon his wife and children and upon his own physical health. Some respondents thought that alcohol exerted a direct effect upon the brain, the sequence going somewhat as follows: taking a few social drinks leads to more drinks, and these drinks have an organic effect upon the brain which then starts up a craving—or alternatively affects the body which starts up the craving—by which time, one way or the other, alcoholism has set in.

By far the largest group of respondents told us that Bill Williams suffered from an error of character; they described him as "no good" and "weak-willed." A very small minority felt that he was drinking to escape some problem which he couldn't face without the use of alcohol and these people urged his need to join Alcoholics Anonymous. Obviously this group approaches the problem differently from the majority. An interestingly large number (40 per cent) said alcoholism is not mental illness because "he is all right in between, and he knows he does wrong." Almost everyone used the term "alcoholic" in their responses; the word appears to have displaced the word "drunkard" in lay vocabularies and the meanings of the two terms seem to have overlapped.

Although responses to the previous histories have suggested that Blackfoot people think mental illness is a condition in which a person seriously and unpredictably contravenes the norms of society, it is clear from the response to this story that such is not the case. One must qualify for the status of mental illness in some further way than just bad behavior!

The next case history, that of Mary White, a phobic girl with compulsive features, follows:

Here's a different sort of girl . . . let's call her Mary White. She seems happy and cheerful; she's pretty, has a good enough job, and is engaged to marry a nice young man. She has loads of friends; everybody likes her; and she's always busy and active. However, she just can't leave the house without going back to see whether she left the gas stove lit or not. And she always goes back again just to make sure she locked the door. And one more thing about her; she's afraid to ride up and down in elevators; she just won't go any place where she'd have to ride in an elevator to get there.

Seventy-two per cent of the respondents said that there was nothing wrong with this girl. A large number of them thought her cautiousness praiseworthy; another large number described it as "just a harmless habit." A substantial group of female respondents exclaimed, "She's just like me!" and many of them described fears in elevators and small spaces with which they had managed to live for years. Many men admitted spontaneously to compulsive behavior similar to that described in this case history "I always used to go back to see that the barn door is shut."

An elevator phobia is explained by Blackfoot citizens as the result of a "scare," another attempt to account for behavior as a rational response which could reasonably have been predicted. There was no respondent who expressed any suspicion that this might be symbolic behavior or that fear of elevators might protect Mary White from other more disturbing unconscious fears. As one might expect, the compulsive behavior relating to the gas stove was immediately recognized as the natural result of Mary White's having caused a fire at one time by not being careful enough in turning off a stove. Apparently Pavlov's influence has been more profound in Blackfoot than has that of Freud!

It was almost unanimously agreed that Mary White was not mentally ill and that her condition, far from being serious, was enviable and praiseworthy. Four per cent thought her mentally ill and 1 per cent thought it was a serious illness. Some respondents became quite irritated with this history. They declared her a perfectly normal person and felt offended that this story was included with tales of drunks and crazy people. In this case, our respondents may well have been correct in their clinical judgment, although some few may have denied what they unconsciously felt to be pathological because it made them anxious. A certain degree of compulsiveness in this society is indigenous; gas stoves are, after all, dangerous; and Mary White is, after all, not complaining of discomfort.

The last case history is that of a delinquent boy.

Now, the last person I'd like to describe is a twelve-year-old boy . . . Bobby Grey. He's bright enough and in good health, and he comes from a comfortable home. But his father and mother have found out that he's been telling lies for a long time now. He's been stealing things from stores, and taking money from his mother's purse, and he has been playing truant, staying away from school whenever he can. His parents are very upset about the way he acts, but he pays no attention to them.

Eighty-three per cent of our respondents said, "Something is wrong," but only 4 per cent thought the boy mentally ill. The great majority argued that the child's parents must have deprived him of sympathy and understanding and perhaps of material things such as spending money. A number of people considered the act of lying in order to escape punishment a normal, healthy reaction to harsh treatment. Woodward[95] reports in an American population the same strong tendency to attribute delinquent behavior in children to rejecting parental attitudes. A very small minority declared that this boy lacked discipline, while another small group attributed it to the effect of either too much or too little discipline; both were seen as damaging. This latter group apparently see "normality" as a condition of being poised precariously between too much and too little, either alternative being very dangerous. The truly impressive fact in the responses is the majority opinion in favor of "softer" child training practices for good emotional development.

The most interesting feature of the responses to this case history is the denial by almost all respondents that this child has a mental illness, on the grounds that "it's not his fault;

it's the fault of the parents; there's something wrong with the parents and nothing wrong with the boy." The implication is strong that mental illness is something generated within a person, and is therefore his own fault. As Bobby Grey's condition is considered to be generated by his parents, he automatically has nothing wrong with him. In brief, there is a tendency in discussing this history to identify the cause with the condition. By the same token, this is not considered a serious condition—because it is not generated within Bobby Grey—except by a minority of respondents who see serious practical problems, such as court convictions, arising if the situation is not dealt with. There is no question of Bobby Grey's having a mental illness in the minds of most of our respondents.

A further striking feature of the responses to this description of a delinquent boy is that the Pavlovian thinking evident in accounting for the elevator phobia tends to be abandoned here. To be consistent, our respondents should either feel that Bobby had not been properly trained (and a tiny minority did say, "He's never been taught the difference between right and wrong") or they should attribute his behavior to rewarding experiences with "bad companions" (and again a very small number did this). The overwhelming majority, however, offered the interviewer what we might call the "mental health approach" of insufficient love, with quite a lot of talk about "it's normal for his age" which strongly suggests certain syndicated columns in newspapers emphasizing the range of behavior to be found in each age-grade. The almost unanimous blame laid upon the parents suggests that the vast modern literature on child training has resulted in the exodus of Pavlovian principles from this area of thought.

One clear over-all impression emerges from the responses to these cases. The definition of a mental illness is much narrower in the minds of the lay public than in the minds of psychiatrists* and the professional mental health workers who conducted the educational program. Our interviewers were shocked at the respondents' denial of pathological conditions in the case histories, because they had assumed that lay people could accept *less* behavior as normal. But a very wide spectrum of behavior appears to be tolerated by the laity—at least verbally†—as reasonably close to normal, and although there was no formal question which could be analyzed to give a definition of mental illness, we found a clear tendency toward operational defining of the mentally ill as "people who have been hospitalized." It was abundantly clear that when our respondents thought of mental illness they thought of psychosis. It is in this sense that we use it in all later analyses.

Clinical experience supports the impression that many people define mental illness as "that condition for which a person is treated in a mental hospital." A case in point is a paranoid woman who came to our attention recently. This patient for some fifteen years had been convinced that she was being influenced by sex rays which came under her bedroom door at night. She suffered also from more transitory delusional beliefs, one of which was that the clergyman of her parish was making counterfeit money in the church basement. Although her delusions were florid in content, there was apparently at no time very much emotion connected with them and she had been successfully employed for many years as a seamstress in a large department store, where she made alterations on clothing. She lived with a sister to whom

* A group of ten psychiatrists commented upon these cases. Although they disagreed among themselves as to the nature of the pathological conditions described, they perceived such conditions much more often than did the Blackfoot respondents.

† Since this was written, a situation has come to our attention in which a man answering almost exactly to that of the paranoid schizophrenic described in our interviews has remained in the community for 20 years and has never been defined as mentally ill, although he has been seriously censured for his behavior.

she habitually confided her ideas, and this sister had always considered her somewhat eccentric. By the time she came under clinical care she was thirty-seven years old, and the reason for her hospitalization was an extended separation from her sister, who had been unexpectedly delayed in returning from a holiday. The patient became anxious at her sister's failure to arrive on schedule and discussed some of her delusions with a friend, who immediately placed her in medical hands. A psychiatrist assessed her, decided against prolonged treatment, and upon making enquiries found that she would be welcomed back to work. Accordingly he discharged her after a short stay in hospital to the care of her sister. However, the sister was very reluctant to have her back, declaring that because she had been in a mental hospital she must be mentally ill and saying, "How do I know what she might do?" This belief in the patient's potential unpredictability troubled the sister seriously, and the psychiatrist's efforts to point out that the patient was just the same as she had always been, that is, perfectly predictable, did not console her. She had not thought of her sister as being mentally ill before, and once this state had been ascribed to her she felt extremely uneasy about taking her back.

The sort of thinking obvious in this example appears to run right through our respondents' replies. Mental illness, it seems, is a condition which afflicts people who must go to a mental institution, but up until they go almost anything they do is fairly normal.* The need to interpret the actions of others as normal is apparently a potent social force.

* Since this study, we have talked with some of the workers in a National Institute of Mental Health family study at St. Elizabeth's Hospital. While their study is not focused on our area, they have been doing extensive interviewing with the families of persons who have been hospitalized for mental illness. They gave us numerous examples of obvious signs of mental illness being rationalized by families until a crucial event forces the realization of illness upon them. At this time, the previous conduct is recognized in retrospect as abnormal and often the first suspicion of illness is dated to a much earlier period than when it actually occurred. For early reporting of this important study see *The Journal of Social Issues,* Vol. XI, No. 4.

Recapitulating, our original assumption that lay people see a narrower range of "normal" behavior than do professionals requires re-examination. It is very likely that this assumption badly misses the mark. What we seem to have discovered is that lay people use a different set of criteria for determining whether or not a person is normal or abnormal than do professionals. Whereas a psychiatrist or other clinically trained person uses specific psychological symptoms to determine not only the presence of abnormality but its severity, the lay person uses normative or moral standards to reach the same conclusion.

Discussing this problem, Lemert says:[46]

It would probably be the consensus of most trained observers of mental disorders that psychotic deviation as described in formal psychiatric categories is not in itself the reason for collective action to bring mentally disturbed persons under restraint. Rather it is the highly visible deviations of the psychotic person from the norms of his group placing strains upon other persons which excite the family or community and cause them to take legal action against him.

That lay and professional people judge "abnormality" along different dimensions is supported by our own mental hospital experience in which patients apparently cured of gross psychological symptoms are sometimes rejected by their relatives as "as bad as ever" while others who are still hallucinated or delusional are occasionally welcomed home as "cured." It appears also that the characteristics which cause people to bring their relatives to hospital are not necessarily those which constitute a set of psychological symptoms. The relationship between those qualities which lay people designate abnormal and psychological symptoms is an incompletely explored area of profound practical importance for the understanding of mental hospital admissions on the one hand and the rehabilitative process on the other.*

* For a more detailed discussion of this point see the authors' "Affective Symbolism, Social Norms, and Mental Illness"—*Psychiatry,* Vol. 19, No. 1.

We realized, in retrospect, that we had assumed, again *implicitly,* that lay people must have professional advice as to the nature of deviant behavior. The error here lies in misunderstanding the nature of society itself. It is scarcely necessary to emphasize that social systems, by definition *equilibrated* systems, have methods of defining deviant behavior without the help of any particular trained body of members. The acceptance of the norms by *all* members ensures that deviance will be recognized and sanctioned by everyone. We still do not know, from our Blackfoot experience, whether lay people tolerate *more or less* deviant behavior in actual fact than do professionals; we only know that they appear to tolerate *different* behavior.

Related to the *implicit* assumption discussed above was the second, and *explicit* working principle, "that behavior is caused and is therefore understandable." This principle appears to have been exactly the same as that used by the Blackfoot population; our problem lay in the fact that we assumed them to be ignorant of it! Furthermore, the "causes" of behavior which we wished to teach these people were in serious disagreement with those which they had worked out for themselves. For example, to most Blackfoot respondents it seems natural that if one is frightened in an elevator in childhood, one will be afraid in elevators in maturity. Dr. Star has told us that this kind of thinking also appears in her American sample. Similarly, if one has received bad treatment in the past, one has reason to feel persecuted now; therefore paranoid behavior has the quality of being "natural." In other words, concrete cause-and-effect thinking about behavior is well established in the minds of our respondents. Our program planning committee displayed naiveté in assuming that people awaited professional advice before deciding upon the specific causes of behavior. As has been pointed out by anthropologists and others,[45, 59] all people come to terms in some way with the "causes" of behavior; and, indeed, common observation should have led us to this conclusion: few people say they do not understand "human nature."

Our attempt to demonstrate that behavior has many symbolic aspects and that cause and effect do not have a simple concrete relationship apparently disrupted a way of thinking about behavior which was quite satisfactory to our respondents. At the same time, the "causes" which our educators incorporated into their material were really clinical opinions derived from reputable schools of psychiatry and psychology, and were not in any real sense "scientific" causes. If we had made the correct assumption that Blackfoot people knew that behavior was caused and then assumed that they were in error as to the nature of the "causes," we might have given more thought to the validity of what we were teaching because our attention would have been focused on the problem of "right" and "wrong" causes. We would have been led to re-examine both our explicit assumption that behavior is caused and can therefore be understood, and our implicit assumption that while *we* knew these causes, the Blackfoot people did not.

Our third working principle, "there is a continuum between normality and abnormality," contained the implication that there is, at best, an arbitrary line between sickness and health. This may be a good theoretical generalization, inasmuch as all individuals undoubtedly experience some leanings toward deviant behavior at one time or another, but it was an unsatisfactory principle for teaching purposes. Our impression is that our respondents saw a fairly sharp cut-off between the mentally well and the mentally ill. This cut-off seems to occur as soon as behavior becomes both non-normative *and* unpredictable. When Blackfoot people are asked to describe a mentally ill person, they frequently describe behavior which makes them anxious, although it may not be *clinically* pathological. The element of unpredictability seems to be a crucial diagnostic point for lay people. Forty per cent of Blackfoot respondents mention it when asked what they mean by mental illness, giving such responses as: "They turn on those they used to love the best," or "If they used to be quiet they act noisy, or if they used to be cheerful they act withdrawn." The suggestion that illness and health fall on a continuous dimension has the concomitant implication that everyone may be a little mad. Such an implication is probably anxiety-producing to people who already have firm, if somewhat unorganized, ideas about the *non-continuous* nature of mental illness.

All in all, it is probably fair to say that the implicit and explicit assumptions underlying our program, and perhaps mental health programs in general, are in part erroneously conceived. The immutability of attitudes regarding mental illness must be in part a function of these misconceptions.

In retrospect, we do not believe that the hostile reaction of the Blackfoot citizens was caused by our *method* of entering the community or of presenting our materials. Furthermore, most mental health education in Canada at that time was being conducted in much the way ours was, and it was the typical, not the atypical, case in which we were interested. It is important that it was the *interviewers,* those who had not been closely associated with the program, who felt the brunt of the hostility. Those who had had close interpersonal contacts in the town, the educational team, at no time received even impolite treatment, let alone outright hostility. The materials which we used were mainly procured from the Canadian Mental Health Association; in fact, the executive secretary of the Provincial Movement was a member of the education planning group. The orientation of the Canadian body is derived directly from the American body, as are its materials. It is unlikely that our materials differed from many of those generally used in mental health programs. We do not believe, in short, that we used atypical method or content in our program.

There is little doubt in our minds that the short space of time in which such a large number of stimuli were applied to the community was a factor in inducing the marked anxiety which we saw. It seems to us quite probable that had we introduced the same material over a much longer period, we would not have had the same flaring reaction at the end of the program. However, the question then becomes, would the anxiety have been absent, or would it have been merely latent if this had been done? More research is needed to clarify this point. In the light of our previous analysis of our assumptions, we now incline to think that the anxiety would have been there, but might have been shown only as apathy or withdrawal.

Similarly, whether the introduction of a service into the community along with the educational material would have made a difference is an open question. It is possible that the introduction of a clinical service might have provided a rationale for our presence in the town which could have deflected anxiety and in some cases alleviated it; it is true that a few people did inquire of the interviewers about the nearest available service. However, it is necessary to distinguish between a program which is intended to introduce a new service into a community, and a program such as ours which was intended to induce a fundamental shift in attitude. Although this requires testing, we are at present inclined to think that the latter endeavor, when based on the type of assumptions which we entertained, is, for the reasons to be discussed in the following chapters, inherently anxiety-producing. There is nothing in our reasoning which suggests that the introduction of a service with an appropriate orientation program would raise anxiety, because such a move —by its nature—does not interfere with the fundamental orientation toward deviant behavior which people hold.

2. *The Salient Findings Reviewed*

Apart from the resistance of the community's attitudes to change, the absolute lowness of the scale scores is interesting in itself. The average person in this community is willing to live in the same neighborhood with former mental hospital patients, but he stops short of "rooming with a former mental hospital patient" and denies willingness for any closer association. That our educational program did not induce our respondents to tolerate closer contact with those who have been mentally ill is evident in a widespread belief, elicited in our post-educational interviews, that they "always show some signs."

Responsibility for mental illness—whether cause or cure —ends, for the average man, with the well-being of his own family and does not quite reach his friends; the average score on the Responsibility Scale corresponds to a point halfway between the item describing responsibility for the immediate family and the item regarding responsibility for friends as well as for family.

Although the mean score had not changed upon resurvey, indicating the over-all stability of this attitude, the change in variance of the Responsibility Scale score among the more highly educated people suggests that this is the more manipulable of the two sets of orientations. It is possible that the relatively neutral concept of responsibility is more amenable to change than is the concept of what sorts of people are suitable for close relationships, especially among middle-class people. It may be easier to persuade such people to agree with the proposition that their community needs mental health guidance than it is to persuade them to agree to assume responsibility for specific classes of people such as fellow-workers. Furthermore, the relative meaninglessness of the phrase "mental health guidance" probably makes it easier for respondents to give "positive" responses to the items containing it. The highly educated group, whose scores seem most sensitive to change, contains those people who are most likely to assign to the phrase "mental health guidance," a meaning which is close to that of the educators.

We conclude that on the whole the people of Blackfoot do not wish to have very much contact with mental illness either on the personal or social level. It is as if they were denying the relevance of the problem of mental health to their lives.

A third finding emerging from this study is the empirical independence of the scores on the two scales. We have discussed the meaning of this finding earlier in this book.

Fourthly, we were impressed with the universality, in the responses to the case histories, of what we will call a "normalizing" theme. This theme, observed first by Dr. Star in her N.O.R.C. sample, consists of a tendency of the respondent to dismiss described psychological symptoms with a phrase such as "It's just a quirk" or "It takes all sorts to make a world." Some respondents deny the seriousness of even the bizarre behavior of the paranoid schizophrenic in these terms. This denial of pathological condition is one of the crucial differences between lay and professional judgments of psychological symptoms, and is, we reiterate, extremely important in the practical care of the mentally ill.*

Finally, the anxiety raised by the program among the citizens of the town suggests that either the approach used in the educational program was threatening or the material

* Questioning of psychiatric nurses in training and recent graduates shows a marked and orderly tendency for the nurse to recognize more and more psychological symptoms as abnormal as her training progresses through time. "Affective Symbolism, Social Norms, and Mental Illness," *op. cit.*

embedded in the program was threatening, or, more probably, that both were true. It is not possible to say which parts of the program produced the anxiety, because it was not manifest until the end and we were not specifically concerned with the effect of the individual items on the list. We may reasonably assume that the interviewing program was not particularly anxiety-producing *per se,* because it had not elicited a hostile reaction when first presented in the autumn. We suspect, as mentioned before, that attempts to legitimate our program as a scientific undertaking produced hostility, especially among the agricultural scientists. It is possible that some people were irritated by our harping upon a subject which was at best peripheral to their interest, and it is also possible that the personality of the chief educator was in some cases an alienating influence—although this last seems unlikely in the light of his success in such enterprises as initiating a psychiatric clinic in a strange community, and conducting an educational program with psychiatric nurses initially hostile to his purpose. But we do not believe that all of these reasons together are sufficient to account for the extent of the community reaction described herein. Later in this book we will discuss what we would do differently if we were conducting another community program, but for the moment we will assume that the results we observed were genuinely related to the content of the program and not solely to the nature of our approach.

In short, it appeared from our interviews that the people of Blackfoot had fixed ideas about the causes of behavior, both normal and deviant, about the proper way to treat the mentally ill, and about the correct amount of responsibility to assume in the matter. Our vigorous attempts to alter these important ideas were unsuccessful and resulted in our co-workers' virtual rejection from the community. We feel, after considerable reflection, that certain concepts regarding the integration of social systems are helpful in accounting for this constellation of facts and are an indispensable adjunct to purely psychological explanations. Therefore in the following section an attempt will be made to organize them in terms of sociological theory. They are presented, not as sole explanations, but as useful, partial explanations.

A Patterned Response
to a Form of Deviance
and an Analysis
of Its Function

1. *The Problem*

So far in this book we have described the result of a specific experiment in mental health education. In our attempt to make a more meaningful interpretation of the results than simply to say "something must have been done wrong" we have called upon other aspects of our clinical and research experience. In this section we shall consider the unchanged attitudes of the Blackfoot people side by side with certain other general information which we have about how they, as well as the rest of Prairie Province, deal with the problem of mental illness at the practical level.

If we place Blackfoot's anxious and hostile reception of our attempt to change their orientation in the context of our specific knowledge that the level of public care of the mentally ill in Prairie Province is not high by any objective standard,* we can consider both facts to be part of a larger, patterned reaction to mental illness in our society. The fact that the somewhat rejecting attitudes of the Blackfoot people toward the mentally ill are so resistant to change together with the uniformity of the substandard treatment of patients in mental hospitals add up to a pattern of behavior which probably has an important latent function for most people. That is to say, the same people who seem so callous in their treatment of the mentally ill—and the indifference of most people to the bad conditions in hospitals is surely callous— must have reasons for their attitudes and actions, because they are not callous people. We will make an attempt here to analyze the meaning of this behavior, using the data from our study, other data which we have collected, general information from our firsthand experience and observation, and evidence derived from the literature.

Although we still use examples known to us, we will assume that the general picture of conditions in mental hospitals is uniform throughout North America, and, as the recurrent phenomenon of the mental hospital exposé suggests, uniform through time also.† We believe that there is a coherent set of reasons for the attitudes toward mental illness which we found in Blackfoot; we believe that these reasons

---

* Not only is this true in Prairie Province, but it is frequently mentioned in the literature. Besides specific exposés such as *The Shame of the States* (Deutsch, 1948), there are more objective accounts: Chapter II of *Social Pathology* (Lemert, 1951) emphasizes the uniformly low level of care of the mentally ill in publicly supported institutions.

† Since this study was undertaken—that is, in the last five years—there has been a tremendous upsurge of interest in conditions in mental hospitals. This seems to have been sparked by two things, the development of a theory of "ward milieu" and discovery of the tranquilizing drugs which have made it possible to calm hitherto intractable patients. We do not yet know whether this burst of interest, like its several predecessors, will end in a sagging back into the miserable "back ward" conditions of the past or whether these two lines of attack will bring permanent relief to the situation. Our analysis is, however, based upon the former assumption, and may therefore err on the gloomy side because of the period in which it was formulated.

are inherent in modern Western society and that the dismaying aspects of treatment of the mentally ill are unintended consequences of people's attempts to render their environment normal and predictable.

In making our analysis we will rely on the model worked out by Merton[52] for tracing the consequences, intended and unintended, of social action.

Many actions which appear to play an important function in maintaining the equilibrium of society have disequilibrating aspects for some of its members or groups of members. Each item of behavior in a society may be thought of as having a "net function," a surplus of equilibrating effect over disequilibrating effect and in some cases even the other way around.

However, before going on to this analysis we will outline as clearly as we can the sociological frame of reference which we are using. We repeat, we do not offer either this frame of reference or the analysis which follows it as a total answer to the many problems created by mental illness, but we do offer it as an important partial explanation of behavior which is frequently overlooked.

We start with the proposition that all societies have certain unwritten rules which people are expected to obey automatically. But people do not act "automatically," so they must somehow be kept behaving as they are expected to, according to the rules. Behavior may be strange, but as long as it is expected it will not be considered abnormally deviant. For example, an adolescent may do bizarre things, but if they are things which are expected of members of the "teen-age set" they are normal, no matter how tiresome they may be. Many adolescents in North America do things which, if judged by European standards, would appear strange to the point of abnormality, but if they are things which are expected—even if somewhat ruefully—of adolescents, they are not deviant, and they are not treated as if they are. Basically, the social problem lies in keeping people *wanting* to honor the expectations of others, motivating them to keep the rules because they *like* to keep the rules.

The never-ending task of keeping people happy when governed by such norms is partly performed by training children to accept other people's expectations of them as right and proper and "natural." Children are carefully trained to feel guilty and unhappy if they break the rules, and this is the result of a deliberate and planned policy on the part of their parents. They are socialized into society with a healthy respect for its norms.

The families of a society have the paramount function of transforming newborn infants into citizens who are equipped with consciences suitable for living comfortably in the community. This process ensures that most of the time most of the people will *want to do what they have to do*. They learn from childhood to feel comfortable when they behave in expected ways and uncomfortable when they do not. They learn too, to expect certain behavior of others and to feel chagrined when it is not forthcoming.

We proceed, therefore, to the proposition that this process of socialization of young children plays a major part in ensuring that norms are honored in society. However, from time to time this process fails. Either the child does not "internalize the norms"—that is, he fails to want to do what is expected of him—or he learns a second set of norms which are inimical to the operation of society as it is constituted. For example he might, for various reasons, learn the norms of a delinquent gang and thus become a "normal" member of a gang which taken as a whole would have to be considered a deviant sector of society.

It is not necessary, of course, that a person who has not fully internalized the norms be unequivocally a deviant.

Some, indeed, are able to belong to what might be called "marginal institutions" which we do not encourage but which we do not actively punish. An example is the artists' colony, not really considered deviant by most people, certainly considered "not done" by a good many, but considered highly desirable by a few. This type of activity, fully acceptable or not, does allow people to straddle the line between expected, normal, acceptable behavior and non-normal, non-acceptable, unexpected behavior.

When an individual does exhibit a clear-cut break with the norms, certain things happen. Members of his subsociety, and possibly all the members of society, will react against his unacceptable behavior. Indeed, they must, because the ordinary, everyday business of social life can only be accomplished if people by and large do what is expected of them and feel guilty and repentant if they fail.

Even a simple act like walking down a crowded street depends for its success upon every person's having thoroughly internalized the rule that one must step sideways to avoid colliding with others. The disconcerting effect of one lurching drunk can demonstrate this point dramatically.

When an individual first shows signs of seriously deviating from the rules, the rest of us usually attempt to control him. First we may make an effort to re-educate him, to persuade him to return to conforming behavior. Perhaps someone has a talk with him: a friend, a brother, a doctor, a clergyman. If this fails and he does not return to conforming behavior, steps may be taken, possibly legal steps, to isolate him so that he may not influence others to think it more rewarding to break the rules than to keep them. He has, after all, magnified the problem many times if he succeeds in forming a small subgroup with rules which are contrary to those of the greater society. If, however, he does form or join such a subsociety and cannot be persuaded to withdraw from it, effective communication between him and the rest of us may be cut off in a kind of insulating process. A penitentiary is a good example of this process. Many of its inmates have gone through the stages mentioned above of "talkings to" and attempted re-education in reformatories before the long-term isolation of the penitentiary has been resorted to.

Compared with the straightforward law-breaking of the criminal, mental illness is a difficult form of deviance for a social system to absorb. It is very hard for us to decide why the mentally ill person behaves as he does; therefore the appeal to him to cease so behaving is difficult. It is easy to attribute a cause to theft (one steals because one wants things), even to crimes of violence; but how does one account for behavior which makes no such sense? In the past, seemingly illogical behavior has been dealt with in ways that then appeared suitable. For many years the problem was settled in quite unequivocal terms; the affected person was possessed by devils. This left no question about the type of control required; those skilled in exorcism, the religious functionaries, were the experts in mental illness, and delusions might well lead to the stake. More recently, however, the control of mental illness has been shared, if somewhat uneasily, between the medical profession and the law.

The treatment of mental illness at the present time is still extremely variable, but whether it is isolation, psychoanalysis, or electric shock, one important function *for society* is the same: to protect the norms and to restore everyday life to the reassuring everyday state where people behave as they are expected to and are happy to do so. On the other hand, the function of treatment *for the individual* is, of course, to cure him of his disorder, and the motive for causing treatment to take place may be entirely that of compassion for the affected person. We are emphasizing the social aspects of mental illness here because it is from the social point of view that we are discussing the problem. This does not mean that our statements are set over against the seemingly quite different statements which are to be found in psychological and psychiatric treatments of the subject, but rather that we believe the social elements should be considered along with the others, not instead of the others. Thus, when we say that a woman's neighbors wish her sent to a hospital because she upsets the equilibrium of society, we take it for granted that they *also* wish her sent to hospital so that she may be treated and thus feel better. As well as wanting to live in a secure social system, people are strongly motivated as a rule to prevent and cure suffering. The business of the psychologist and the psychiatrist is to understand, prevent, and cure suffering, but the business of the sociologist is to examine the relationship between suffering and the social systems in which it occurs: the family, the neighborhood, and the community.

We are, then, concerned with mental illness as a form of deviance which upsets the equilibrium of the society in which it occurs. We are not concerned with mental illness as a condition which various people experience in different ways, but rather with the reaction of the other members of society to the person who has become ill. Our approach is complementary to that of psychiatry and psychology. Specifically we are describing the reactions of the people of a small town to an attempt to change the quality of their thinking about mental illness, and the collective behavior of the people of a Canadian province in caring for their mentally ill.

In the course of our story we will try to demonstrate that the people of the community we studied have a kind of patterned reaction to mental illness, and that this pattern had a place in the general social life.

2. *The Patterned Items*

We have listed below some items of behavior toward mental illness of which we have general information and to which we impute a function. These items are all part of a pattern of values, beliefs, and behavior which we shall call "denial, isolation, and insulation of mental illness in this society." We believe that they play a vital role in maintaining expectations, even though they may appear callous as they are stated here. They are:

1. The rejection of homecoming patients by the community. As we mentioned before, the task of getting reacceptance for mental hospital patients is very often a difficult one for social workers, and there is evidence that this is universally so.[78] Findings from our interviews suggest a certain level of awareness of this problem in Blackfoot; when asked to discuss the general problem of mental illness, 25 per cent of our respondents mentioned rejection as a factor in relapse or spoke of the need for public education to "remove the stigma" from mental illness.

2. The condition of large state-supported mental hospitals in all of North America has been repeatedly documented. In Prairie Province the level of staff is high both in numbers and quality, but they work in badly designed and inconvenient hospitals, housing a total of 4,000 patients, which are, by American Psychiatric Association Standards, 100 per cent overcrowded.* No public indignation attends this deplorable situation despite the fact that these patients are *almost all related to other citizens of the Province.* Even the findings of a Royal Commission recently engaged in investigating one of these hospitals created little interest. Many states in the United States have similar situations.

3. The social and physical isolation of the 4,000 patients in the two Prairie Province mental hospitals. In the first place, both hospitals are in the country, far from the major

* This condition is improved since the time of writing—see the authors' "Improving Patient Care through Social Reorganization." *Psychiatry,* Vol. 19, No. 3.

urban centers. On one ward of 110 men, averaging fifteen years in hospital, we found from the records that no patient received visitors as often as once a month, 10 or 15 had visitors once or twice a year, and the remainder have no visitors at all. The doctor in charge of the ward reports that he receives about six letters a week regarding the men on this ward, and occasionally a personal letter comes for a patient. We calculate that an average of three letters per year per man is received by the hospital and two out of three of these are addressed to the hospital authorities and are concerned with purely legal or administrative matters. This particular ward is not badly "deteriorated" but is in fact rather typical of a "better" chronic ward, clean and orderly, shown to visitors. It has, however, neither clock nor calendar in its day rooms, and those few men who habitually converse together do not know each other's names. All patients wear hospital clothing rather than their own; there is an air of timeless anonymity about this chronic ward. Letters in the files of these patients sometimes contain such requests as, "If my husband is not going to get better please tell me so as I wish to marry again." Would it be possible to get any closer to the role of a dead person? Physical isolation and social isolation are inseparably linked in mental illness.

This three-item list does not pretend to exhaust the pattern of isolation of mental illness; it is only an example of the sorts of behavior readily visible to those working in any field related to the large mental hospital. We shall now list some items specifically derived from our Blackfoot experience:

(a) The rejection by the citizens of Blackfoot of our attempt to change their attitudes toward mental illness.

(b) The content of the items concurred in by the Blackfoot citizens on both the Responsibility and Distance scales. This suggests a strong disinclination on the part of our respondents to be associated with the problem of mental illness in any form. Probably the fact that only 32 per cent of our respondents were able to imagine themselves becoming mentally ill indicates a denial of the relevance of the problem. Combining these two data, we make a tentative interpretation of a tendency to deny the reality of mental illness as a social fact relevant to everyday life.

(c)   The presence in almost all responses of a "normalizing theme." This response of immediate denial of any inherent problem in described deviant behavior suggests that there may be a more general tendency to deny, at least upon first confrontation, the existence of deviant behavior.

(d)   The frequent statement, made to our interviewers, that mental hospitals are excellently run and highly therapeutic for the mentally ill, found together with a contradictory expression of doubt as to whether the patients ever recover. In all, 54 per cent of our respondents thought either that most patients remain ill or that only about half of them get better.

Following up this point we find that upon being asked outright whether mentally ill patients ought to be sent to mental hospitals, 49 per cent of the members of our sample said that they ought to be because mental hospitals have the "finest treatment available." Many described a skilled staff of people trained in the expert handling of the mentally ill. Some respondents declared it downright unfair to deprive the mentally ill of such facilities. Only 9 per cent were totally opposed to hospitalization, although 14 per cent felt it should be resorted to only if the patient were violent. The fact that the mental hospitals of Prairie Province were at this time grossly overcrowded and seriously lacking in therapeutic facilities and therapeutic programs makes this an extremely interesting response. One Blackfoot citizen said to the interviewer, "Well, I think the mental institutions have it down to a fine art. If anyone can cure them, they can. They don't ignore them, they really go to town on them. These mental institutions can do wonders." Apparently exposés of publicly supported mental hospitals have not been read in Blackfoot and films like *The Snakepit* have not been seen. This belief in the efficacy of mental institutions seems even more certainly part of a pattern when it is combined with the fact that the majority, 85 per cent, of the people holding it stated during their interviews that they had known or then knew someone in a mental hospital. It seems extremely unlikely that the people they had known told them of the excellence of the hospital; some other reason for believing in it must have been present; perhaps it was a pressing need to deny the existence of a problem.

In patterned behaviors perceived in the Blackfoot material there is implied a sequence of events: the denial of deviance, followed, when denial is no longer possible, by a movement toward isolation of the deviant both socially and physically; and, finally, insulation, a denial that the isolated deviant is a problem. Furthermore, as we have said, there is a tendency for our respondents to feel that the mentally ill either will not get better at all or will always show some signs of their illness, and this provides a thrust toward insulating them from society.

In summary, the social response to mental illness seems to be: first, denial of mental illness; second, isolation of the affected person in a hospital when mental illness can no longer be denied, with concomitant rationalization of this isolation with beliefs that the hospital is a wonderful place, capable of curing mental illness, if it can be cured at all, which is doubtful; and, finally, insulation of the whole vexing problem by a secondary denial that a problem exists insofar as it needs solving by ordinary citizens.

An example of the isolating mechanism will illustrate the force with which it operates. A confused and anxious gentleman in his sixties, brought to hospital by his son, a farmer, was received into the admitting ward of a mental hospital. The son, a middle-aged man, did not visit the hospital again until he was requested to do so by the attending doctor. When he came he refused to see his father, giving as his reason, "Well, I don't want to visit him, it would just upset him. I know he is much happier here." Many such examples could be given in which the move to isolate the patient rests on a stated desire to achieve the patient's best welfare, a statement which, as in the above instance, cannot bear careful inspection. Specifically, the son of our patient had no objective, rational cause for thinking his father would be happy in the mental hospital, and it is quite possible that he had several latent reasons for thinking quite the opposite; but his need to isolate his deviant and no doubt troublesome father was sufficient to allow him to bring him to hospital; finally, his thrust to deny the problem of having expelled his father from the family led him to express the belief that isolation in a mental hospital would make him happier! This man, furthermore, is tacitly saying, as our Blackfoot respondents did, "The hospital can cure, but unfortunately the patient can't be cured."

(e)   A very important item in the isolation pattern resides in certain inconsistencies of response to inquiries about feeling about meeting someone who had been mentally ill. To the question, "If you found out that someone you knew who seemed all right now had been in a mental hospital once, do you think you'd feel any different about being around this person?" a majority of 74 per cent said that they would feel *no* differently while 24 per cent said that they would feel differently, mostly more solicitous and tactful.

When the answers of the 74 per cent who claimed they would feel no differently are scrutinized, however, it transpires that two-thirds of them feel that others would, unlike themselves, reject, fear, or even ridicule someone who had been mentally ill. It is highly probable that this group, 43 per cent of the total number of respondents, is describing its own latent feelings. The most common response, "I'd feel no differently . . . others would be afraid because they would always be watching for him to go off again," indicates that the perceived instability and unpredictability of those who have been mentally ill is a crucial factor in producing anxiety about associating with ex-patients of mental hospitals.

Twenty-three per cent of the survey sample said that they would feel no differently and neither would others; and 21 per cent gave what is probably the most realistic response, that they would feel somewhat nervous and so would other people.

The majority seem to feel the need to state, although in a somewhat hypocritical way, that they would feel no differently, indicating a certain marked degree of institutionalization of the value, "mental illness is nothing to be ashamed of," but an institutionalization that is only skin deep; it seems to rest uneasily upon a genuine feeling of dismay.

The people who claimed to have known a person who had been mentally ill did not answer these questions differently from those who said they had not, suggesting that it is a moral and social area of attitude rather than a specific, personal, and idiosyncratic one. Personal experience, in other words, does not influence or modify these beliefs.

Toward the end of this interview a question was asked which is related to this area of analysis: "Do you think that you would like to see a psychiatrist?" Almost everyone replied, "Yes, if I had anything wrong with me," explaining that they would know when something was wrong that required psychiatric attention. A few answered a firm "No," saying, "I can handle my own problems." Our guess is that "mental illness is nothing to be ashamed of" sits uneasily here too, as perhaps it does with all of us, and that what is really meant is "other people's mental illnesses are nothing for *them* to be ashamed of; with me it is a different question."

All in all, this item of behavior seems to point to a fear and rejection of people who have been defined as mentally ill which is half hidden by an uncomfortable conviction that it is wrong to feel this way.

(f) A final item for our list of evidences for a tendency to deny, isolate, and insulate mental illness comes from the answers to the last question in the Blackfoot interview schedule. Here the respondents are asked what should be done about ". . . the large amount of mental illness in the country." Responses to this question are remarkable for their poverty. Only a few people have more than one suggestion, and "I don't know" is an almost automatic beginning. When probed, most say that they guess *more* facilities are the answer. This question found people at a genuine loss, and this we construe as a denial of the problem. The answers seem to mean, first there is nothing to be done, and second, if something is wrong, more of what we are doing at the moment is the best answer. It is as if our respondents said, "This is not my problem."

We have presented certain selected evidences that the social response to mental illness is one of denial, isolation, and insulation, but we have not yet attempted to deal with the question, "Why is this so?" In some respects, it is obvious, this pattern closely parallels the response to criminal behavior. Both attempt to isolate and insulate the deviant from society by keeping him in an institution, yet there is no precedent for believing that the mentally ill do, or even can, form subsocieties which recruit new members and thus threaten us in the way that delinquents do. We must assume that the threat of mental illness lies elsewhere than in dangerous group action. There is, it is true, some evidence that under special conditions certain popular and charismatic leaders such as Hitler have been clinically or legally insane, but the powerful subsocieties which form around them are primarily of *non-deviant* people. There is no evidence that mentally ill people are capable of the effective group action of delinquents and criminals, whom society isolates *partly* to prevent formation of subsocieties. In short, there is a danger of criminals banding together to perform dangerous criminal acts, but there is no danger of psychotics banding together to perform acts of lunacy.

Having discussed at some length the items making up a patterned response to mental illness, we turn to the question of why people feel prompted to behave in this patterned manner.

3. *The Motivation*

The motive for any particular pattern of behavior need not correspond with the function which that behavior has for society. For example, although people's behavior toward the mentally ill has the end result of isolating them, this is not the motive behind the behavior. Durkheim, discussing the function of criminal law, observed that the *motive* for isolating criminals is punishment of the crime but the *function* is the affirmation of the integration of the law-abiding society. He says,[25] "It is the common conscience which is attacked, and it must resist and the resistance must be collective." Similarly, while the motive for isolation in mental illness is no doubt the treatment of the ill, the latent function is the reaffirmation of the solidarity of the social system in which the norms are not violated—*the solidarity of the sane.*

4. *The Functions of the Pattern, Manifest and Latent*

There are often unintended and unrecognized consequences of behavior. We will examine the pattern we have described, and which for convenience we will refer to hereafter as simply "the isolation pattern," for signs of such consequences. The total society as well as the smaller subsociety of the mental hospital and its patients are affected by these consequences. If we take the greater community and its welfare as the point of reference we can see both good and bad results of the pattern; the following positive functions appear to be performed by the isolation pattern.

(a) An intended and recognized function of the isolation pattern is the attempt to restore the individual to a state of health. There is no question that mental hospitals are able to do this for about 75 per cent of the patients admitted. This function coincides exactly with the expressed motive for the pattern. However, it has never been firmly established just how many patients would recover spontaneously without the ministrations of the hospital, and if indeed more would not recover were there no hospitals. However, hospitalization is probably instrumental in "curing" a good many patients, especially those suffering from depressions and from acute schizophrenia. The term "cure" is used here to mean that the disease is in remission; this is the same sense in which the word is used by other branches of the medical profession.

(b) A second intended and recognized function of the isolation pattern is the protection of the community from the small percentage of the mentally ill who are violent and present a real danger.

As well as these two manifest and intended functions for the greater community, there appear to be certain latent functions of the isolation pattern, of which the following two may well be crucial:

(a) Probably the more important latent function is, as we have adumbrated, the maintenance of the integration of the community as a predictable and normative social system. In other words, as long as a member's behavior can be tolerated and labelled as "sane," he will be treated as a functioning member of the community. Because expectations have such a strong influence upon everyone, there will be a tendency for people who are labelled as sane to behave sanely. The expectation of continuing sanity tends to slow up the development of deviant behavior and therefore the loss of members from the community. It is quite possible that the denial of deviance may, in a number of cases, provide sufficient time for a spontaneous remission to take place, and thus prevent the loss of a member.

However, once deviant behavior reaches a stage where its manifestations are undeniable—probably where "unpredictability" and "non-normativeness" are at some level recognized and the label "mental illness" is applied—society must respond with isolation against the threat of behavior which is ungoverned by the rules. So it is that the physical and social isolation of mentally ill people serves to preserve the expectation that members of society will, day after day, act out their roles in an orderly and understandable way. The solidarity of the sane is reaffirmed through the alienation in a very concrete sense of those who threaten it. Recalling our Blackfoot experience, our educational program not only implicitly reproved people for protecting their solidarity through the isolation of the mentally ill but it further undermined this important latent function by implying that there is very little need for a special set of attitudes toward mental illness on the grounds that the mentally ill are very little different from the mentally well.

(b) A second latent function is performed by the "insulation" part of the isolation pattern. To begin with, there can be little question that a person who sends someone with whom he has a close relationship into a mental hospital suffers remorse over having exiled that person from his family or friendship group. To be able to deny that a problem exists probably alleviates this feeling.* Ironically, social workers and physicians in hospitals often find that one of their chief functions with regard to relatives is relieving this guilt, thus, no doubt, legitimizing the "it's the best place for him" defense which already exists. As social workers and physicians are themselves carriers of the values of the societies in which they live, this reinforcement function is not surprising. The em-

---

* It can be argued that the reduction of guilt is better termed "adjustive for the individual," than "functional for the social system."[45] However, if the phenomenon in question is relevant to a large segment of society, as we believe this one to be, the two concepts tend to overlap because clearly guilt-ridden members cannot be considered functional for our type of society.

phasis of our program upon the undischarged obligation of people and communities to these hospitals and the incidental discussions of conditions in them must have interfered seriously with this guilt-reducing function.

5. *The Unintended Consequences to the Greater Community*

From the point of view of the greater community, the pattern of isolation has some serious unintended and unrecognized malfunctional, or disequilibrating, consequences which are in sharp contrast with both of the two recognized and intended functions of curing patients and protecting the greater community, as well as with the two unrecognized and unintended functions of reaffirming the solidarity of the social system and reducing the guilt of its members.

(a) An immediately obvious malfunction of the isolation pattern is the loss to the community of a large number of individuals, many of whom, even with their illnesses, could be producing members of society. This represents a concrete loss of many millions of dollars a year. At the same time, there is the concomitant loss of the personnel who attend the mentally ill, some of whom are among the most highly trained members of society. There is a vicious-circle quality to this malfunction, inasmuch as it has been reasonably demonstrated that expectations have a great deal to do with the curing of patients.[82] Ward staff members, whose pessimistic views about the prognosis of their patients represent in many ways those of the general population, are themselves one of the forces acting against the recovery of the patients. Thus we have a circular process which tends to perpetuate this loss.

(b) A second malfunction for society resides in the physical isolation of the mental hospital. The inaccessibility and "mysteriousness" of these places inhibits the demand for early medical treatment of emotional disorders. While we have no convincing scientific evidence that early treatment does indeed prevent mental illness, the assumption that it does is at the basis of clinical practice, and therefore anything militating against it must be counted a malfunction. We have said above, however, that the delayed recognition of mental illness which prevents early treatment is a *function* for society, and later we will contend for the individual, and it must be recognized that there may be both good and bad aspects of failing to secure early treatment in many cases. Researches into the efficacy of early treatment versus treatment after the onset of acute illness would help us to decide whether early treatment does more harm by needlessly stamping some people as "mentally ill" than it does good by improving prognosis.

(c) A further malfunction of the physical isolation of the mentally ill is its effect upon the recruitment of professional workers. Good doctors, social workers, psychologists, and so on do not wish to be cut off from the ongoing currents of professional life.[7] Again, a vicious circle is evident; the marginal people who are so often attracted to mental hospitals[46] further the isolation pattern by lowering the recovery rate.

6. *The Functions of the Pattern for the Mentally Ill*

When we turn our attention away from the community and examine the pattern from the perspective of the patients themselves, we can detect in the isolation pattern two clear-cut recognized and intended functions.

(a) Leaving aside whether or not the patient wants to recover, and assuming that it is a good thing if he does, we recognize that the treatment facilities which are available to newly admitted patients in most mental hospitals probably hasten the remission of the disease process. We cannot be sure, but we believe treatment in a mental hospital favors recovery in many instances.

(b) Hospitalization does act as a protection from self-directed violence for many patients, and it also protects them from the consequences of their own outer-directed violence which might in the end cause them a great deal of difficulty. Similarly, they are protected from the extreme sanctions which might be brought to bear on them by the community, were they not hospitalized. Thus the isolated hospital does protect and treat the patient in a situation of minimum interference.

As well as these two manifest and intended functions for the patient, at least two latent and unintended consequences appear reasonably certain.

(a) Hospitalization removes the patient from the sources of stress which may have precipitated his disease or aggravated his non-conforming behavior. This function is usually not intended by any of the persons involved in the patient's removal, and it almost never is given primacy. Anyone who has worked in large mental hospitals has seen new patients in states of agitation apparently brought about by their immediate environment become calm quite soon after admission.

(b) Denial of the presence of abnormality has the important latent function of allowing some deviant behavior to take place without a label being attached to it. This permissiveness is an important "safety-valve" for people who are temporarily under stress, protecting them from being labelled "mentally ill." Although this same pattern militates against early treatment, it is possible that the net effect is functional if it prevents a vicious circle from developing through the labelling of marginal behavior as mental illness, and the subsequent expectation of non-normative behavior.

7. *The Unintended Consequences to the Mentally Ill*

As well as the two latent functions just described, the isolation pattern has serious *unintended malfunctional* consequences for the mentally ill themselves, of which some are described below.

(a) A serious malfunction of the pattern of isolation is the failure of a large number of patients to recover. This failure is related to the expectation by the members of society, as documented in Blackfoot, that the patient will not get well. There is no question that patients are aware of this expectation. Again, the ward staffs caring for the patients bring the patterns of the greater population with them to their work.* Apparently these patterns are intensified in them by contact with the mentally ill. These people appear, from preliminary evidence, to undergo a curious process in which they learn to defend themselves against the threat of the hospital environment by a psychological rejection and isolation of the patients. Our preliminary studies suggest that the difficulty

---

* In a later experiment we discovered that ward staffs do differ from the public, but that they are much closer to them in attitudes and beliefs than they are to professionals of higher training such as psychiatrists and psychologists.

encountered in training mental hospital staffs is caused in part by the following interrelated factors: Although the best training experience for the staff is to see the patients recover under their ministrations, the chances for their recovery are greatly reduced by a pessimistic belief that they will not get better. It is plain that a number of factors converge to overdetermine the great numbers of chronic mental hospital patients.

(b) A second unintended consequence of the actual physical isolation of mental hospitals lies in the kind of neglect which is possible when public inspection is lacking. For example, the frequent failure of ward staffs to keep patients properly clothed is partly a function of the remoteness of the hospital from the public gaze. Further, this remoteness, with its lack of contacts with ongoing society, means that the patient who does recover after protracted hospitalization will resocialize in a curiously aberrant social system and will have no opportunity while in hospital to become reintegrated with the kind of social system to which he will return. This discontinuity can well be thought of as a serious strain in the rehabilitative process often leading to relapse.

There are, all in all, a number of sadly circular effects of the isolation pattern which tend to depress the status of the mentally ill person and to lessen his chances for recovery. These are the unintended by-products of the intended and manifest functions of protecting society and treating the patient. While everyone recognizes and approves his duty to society, many regret that the cost is so high.

Theoretical Implications
of the Pattern

We have hitherto based our discussions fairly closely upon our specific findings in Blackfoot and our experience in our work. We now turn to more general but nonetheless important considerations of mental health programs which are related to our findings.

Our analysis of some of the manifest and latent functions of the isolation pattern raised one very important question. Are there inevitably "bad" consequences lurking beneath well-intentioned stable patterns of behavior? And, more specifically, does the solidarity of the sane have to hinge upon the isolation of the mentally ill? In part these questions must be answered by researches which attempt some kind of measurement of the balance between the functions and the malfunctions of the pattern. However, to a very important extent, they involve value judgments based on social ethics rather than upon scientific considerations; and therefore their answer becomes more difficult—or more easy depending upon the point of view—and tends to depend on the kind of ideal society we have in mind.

Perhaps an answer to our question lies in asking, "What patterns of reaction to mental illness would perform an integrative function for the members of society without being so malfunctional for the mentally ill?" We cannot fully answer this question without further research, but the following pages present some tentative answers.

Society must at all times remain in some kind of equilibrium or it loses its integrity and ceases to be a system. As we have said earlier, the fundamental basis of this equilibrium in a stable society is the members' desire to act most of the time in ways expected of them. This "complementarity of expectations"[60] is disrupted in mental illness; the affected person appears no longer to be governed by the norms which apply to his fellows. He seems insensitive to the expectations of those around him. He has, therefore, in a very real and crucial way, broken his ties with society. He appears no longer to be bound by the expectations which govern the rest of us; he has slipped out of the web of obligations and privileges which bind together conforming members, and therefore he poses a problem of control. And the need for control raises the question, can a member of society break the rules and not be punished? All societies punish deviants in one way or another because the implications of *not* punishing them threaten the stability of society. As the great sociologist Emile Durkheim[25] perceived, it is not entirely to punish the criminal that punitive action is taken but rather to allow the remaining members to reassure one another that they are members of a society which is safe from deviant tendencies.

However, it has become untenable to punish the mentally ill, because the modern, rational, scientific approach has led us to define the mentally ill person as a sick person, and the question then becomes: is it right to punish the sick? This is the dilemma which people face when they attempt to make up their minds about mental illness, and this is one dilemma that the pattern of denial, isolation, and insulation helps to resolve.

A second dilemma arises when we come to define the role which a mentally ill person is expected to play. The role of the physically ill person,[64] on the other hand, is quite well understood in our society, but, as we have illustrated earlier, the specification of the "mentally ill" role which exists in the minds of lay people is in some ways complicated, contradictory, and very hard to verbalize. Again the implicit problem arises, are the mentally ill really ill in the same way as the physically ill, or are they something else? If they are ill why don't they try to get better? Why don't they seek competent help and cooperate with the doctor as the physically ill do? In short, do they really accept the role of "sick patient" and try to get better? The psychiatrist may say that they cannot try to get better because they are mentally ill; in short, that the nature of mental illness forbids the effort, but the question then shifts to: "Can one stretch the meaning of the word 'ill' to cover this kind of behavior?" The delinquent does not try to mend his ways; is he ill too? It is the nature of the *limits* of the sick role that trouble us when we think of mental illness.

We all know what happens to a person who claims the privileges of the sick role and then fails to cooperate with others' attempts to get him better. He soon gets cast into the role of "malingerer" and "lead swinger" (or perhaps, if he belongs to the middle class, "hypochondriac"). However, to return to the role of the mentally ill, if he is not sick, and he sometimes doesn't seem to conduct himself as if he were, what is he? That he is deviant is certain because he throws the interaction processes of society out of equilibrium, but if he doesn't ask for help must we bear with him or should he be dealt with?

Undoubtedly there are requirements in any social system which make it necessary to do something about people who are grossly disoriented and disturbed. Those who have, for whatever reason, lost normative contact with their fellow men are at least temporarily unable to utilize the patterns which they internalized during their early training in their families, and must, therefore, have some substitute for these patterns. Society certainly has to be protected from people who are potentially violent, and from people who are genuinely unpredictable; in short, from physical and symbolic disruption. However, a good deal more than the intended functions are being served by the isolation pattern. If there is to be a better way of dealing with the mentally ill, we must examine the specific ways in which the present method operates in order to know where to make the changes. Our evidence points to three social mechanisms through which the isolation pattern is acted out.

The first is by defining the role of the mentally ill* person in a certain way. A summarizing definition from the Blackfoot material might be that "mental illness is a state of motivated unpredictability and non-normativeness for which a person is treated in a mental hospital." However, in reality, once the mentally ill person comes to a large mental hospital he is redefined as a "patient" and these hospitals we know have ways of defining the role of patient and influencing the patient's behavior in that role which make him predictable. The staffs in these hospitals do not wish to deal with unpredictable people any more than do any other group, and they are in a position to exercise serious, and

* A fuller discussion of this subject is contained in the authors' paper "Affective Symbolism, Social Norms and Mental Illness," *Psychiatry*, Vol. 19, No. 1.

sometimes violent, sanctions against the mentally ill if they do not behave in the patient role as defined. Although the exact definition of the role of mental hospital patient is largely unexplored, some studies done in smaller hospitals give reason for believing that if a patient remains any length of time in hospital, he will be *rendered* predictable by the staff, probably through some invidious process of desocialization. In conclusion, the public definition "the mentally ill person" and the ward staff definition "mental hospital patient" are geared together in a way which renders the patient socially unacceptable at some level, and may be said to be important mechanisms whereby the isolation pattern is acted out.

A second way of acting out the pattern is through devaluation of the large mental hospital, its patients, and its staffs. There is much general evidence for this phenomenon. Anyone who has worked in such an institution is accustomed to the surprise expressed by some lay people that mental hospital psychiatrists are "real doctors." The public apathy about the condition of mental hospitals is reflected in the level of public financial support given to them. Blackfoot closed its ranks against us when we tried to change its convictions in this matter.

The third important social mechanism for the acting out of the physical isolation of the mental hospital patient is the legal right of remand. A mentally ill person can, in most parts of the Western world, be taken against his will into care in an institution. Control over his affairs can be invested in the state without his consent. It must be re-emphasized, however, that while this legal pattern has the unfortunate effect of fortifying and legitimizing the isolation of the patient, it undoubtedly plays an important role in the protection of the community and of the patient.

There must be other ways whereby mental illness is denied

in its early stages, later isolated, physically and symbolically, from the greater society, and finally expelled, even as a problem. Exploration of these mechanisms and of the ways in which people live with them comfortably is important for any discussion of alternative methods of handling mental illness, because whatever functions these mechanisms perform in society must also be performed by the equivalents.

A functional equivalent of any item in a society is one which, although different, does the same job. The difficulty in trying to design functional equivalents of the isolation pattern lies in maintaining intact its useful qualities while getting rid of its harmful ones. For example, only a very few mentally ill people are potentially violent and therefore need to be physically isolated, but how can we separate these few from that great majority who are not in any sense a physical danger? Unfortunately we are hampered by the fact that mental illness is classified on medical principles: the word "schizophrenia" tells us something about a personality, but does not really tell us anything specific about behavior and still less about *why* a particular act is considered abnormal or dangerous by others in society. It would be helpful in thinking about ways of improving the treatment of mental illness if we were able to describe certain forms of it in social-control terms. For example, one category might be of "people who do not feel impelled to behave in expected ways" or "people who are unable to discern what is expected of them."* This kind of classification might very well lead to much closer estimates of the danger of certain groups of patients than is now possible.

Functional equivalents of the isolation pattern would certainly have to retain the quality of protecting society from

---

* Lemert,[46] a sociologist, says of this problem: "it may be asked . . . whether the stumbling block impeding sociological research on mental disorders . . . is not the failure to work out a system of definitions and classifications which have sufficient sociological relevance."

these few dangerous people, but classification of mental illness based on the way the affected person interacts with others might enable us to make an effective separation of the few dangerous from the many harmless patients.

Digressing, it is of interest that suicide, although commonly committed by depressed or paranoid people, is not commonly looked upon as a sign of mental illness. Woodward[95] reports a study similar to the Blackfoot interviewing program in which a case history describing a man who had attempted suicide was read to respondents and only 2 per cent of them thought that he needed psychiatric care. Most of the remainder said that his friends, family, or physician should give him a "pep talk." Self-directed violence is not mental illness to the lay person, even though it is always considered pathological by the professional. At the same time, while suicide is catastrophic for family and friends, it is not essentially as disruptive to the larger community as much outwardly directed violence, and this may account for its exclusion from the deviant category.

Returning to the immediate problem of functional equivalents for the isolation pattern, the following two are offered very tentatively in an effort to indicate possible steps in improving the lot of the mentally ill.

Firstly, if a small group of the mentally ill could legitimately be defined as potentially disruptive to the social system, it might be possible to declare isolation of this small group to be a precaution taken in the interest of society. This process would be an analogue to the well-established practices of physical medicine. Here, illnesses are clearly handled in terms of their potential threat to the community. The most persistently dangerous, such as tuberculosis patients, are isolated in sanatoria, while those of more transitory menace are isolated temporarily in contagious diseases hospitals. People with grievous illnesses like heart lesions who present no threat are not sent away from the community.

If a similar type of classification could be worked out for mental illness, the motive and function of the isolation pattern could remain the same. Such a policy would of course involve a great change in the orientation of the professional mental health worker. It would mean a removal of much mental illness from its position as a subtype of physical illness. The establishment of a separate treatment unit for those who are dangerous, such as the Institution for Criminal Psychopaths, at Herstedvester pr. Glostrup, Denmark, is undoubtedly such a first step. This institute, which attempts to resocialize dangerously ill patients, and contains them if it cannot, has now operated with considerable success for many years, and it is surprising that it is not more widely emulated. Denmark has the smallest percentage of its population in mental hospitals of any Western European country, and one can justifiably ask if it is not because the dangerous group has been weeded out that this is possible. The classification problem inherent in this approach is certainly one for psychiatrists, but the reorientation of the public to such a program is within the province of mental health workers, and their role will be discussed in the next section.

A functional equivalent of the isolation pattern which is complementary to the one above is the complete foster home care of the mentally ill. This type of care has important historical precedents. There is in Belgium the town of Gheel[43] in which traditionally the mentally ill have lodged in the homes of the townspeople. In medieval times, the Irish Princess Dymphna is said to have been slain there by her insane father, who wished to marry her. Because she let him murder her rather than accept his incestuous offer, she was beatified. Later a shrine was erected in her name because she was thought to have "strength" against madness—it was assumed that because he felt incestuous desire, her father was mad. Soon people began to come to

Gheel with their demented relatives to pray for divine intercession, and, while they were there, they lodged in the homes in the town. Eventually Gheel became famous for its religious cures. Today people are treated in a modern treatment unit to which they go by day, returning at night to the homes in which they lodge. The people of Gheel are the landlords of the mentally ill and thus do not act out an isolation pattern. Instead they interact with mentally ill people in a certain specified relationship, that of landlord and tenant. This obviously is, and can be, a functional equivalent of the isolation pattern. Several interesting foster home care plans in the United States, notably one in New York State, have been described;[16] but the problems involved in introducing this equivalent on a large scale into a modern industrialized society which has no such tradition may be manifold. Nevertheless, it would undoubtedly be very profitable to consider the Belgian and the Danish models when planning reform in the treatment and care of the mentally ill on this continent.

It is possible that several fundamental features of our type of society will always make change in our pattern of reaction to mental illness difficult to bring about.

In the first place, small modern families live in small houses and apartments and need to be mobile both physically and socially. They find it very difficult to care for relatives who have any degree of impairment of their abilities. There has been a decline in the practice of keeping aged or ill people in the home. It is no longer considered entirely improper to hospitalize or institutionalize any family member who is unable to "carry his weight" or who seriously hinders the ability of others to do so. Generally speaking the accepted value has become the *care* of the infirm and the ill; and, especially where there are small children, this need not be in the home. It is not always considered "fair" to young people that they should be "handicapped" by looking after their aging parents. It is sometimes felt that "they have their own lives to live." Here "the hospital is the best place for them" performs a real function. A functional equivalent might very well lie in supporting the home in which illness occurs, both financially and emotionally.

A second feature of our society which might make change difficult is the widespread belief in scientific medical practice and therefore in the hospitalization of the ill. The care and treatment of the mentally ill lies almost exclusively in the hands of the medical profession—although neither logic nor tradition indicate conclusively that this is necessarily its only suitable place. The psychiatric branch of medicine is not as closely tied to the exact sciences as are most others, and therefore it is singularly difficult for a doctor specializing in psychiatry to assume the role of scientific healer to the same degree as a doctor specializing in medicine or surgery. Therefore, it is hard for the psychiatrist to legitimize his methods in the same way as, for example, a surgeon does. He may be anxious because he is attempting to deal with problems that he does not clearly understand. He just does not know as much about the psyche as the surgeon knows about the soma. This strain in the practice of psychiatry makes it easier for a doctor to treat his patients in a hospital than in the home where he must maintain a relationship with the anxious family on the basis of his special ability to "do something" for the patient. In a sense, the family trusts him "because he is a scientist," but he cannot himself feel this confident of his ability as a "scientist," and as a result, a strain in the relationship between the doctor and the family makes hospitalization of the mentally ill more agreeable to the doctor. This in turn reinforces the isolation pattern.

These two aspects of modern society are only examples of the types of beliefs and practices which operate against major changes. Comparison with more traditional, stable, and "conserving" societies like Sweden and Norway might be very fruitful.

Whenever a patterned reaction has serious latent malfunctional consequences, the question must be asked, "How are these malfunctions contained within the structure of society?" That is, "Why doesn't someone *do* something about it if it's so bad?" Certainly in the case of the isolation of the mentally ill we have managed to contain the pattern fairly adequately over a long period of time, although not without a certain discomfort. In our experience people visiting crowded mental hospital wards for the first time are almost always horrified; they exhibit a "Why isn't something done about it?" reaction.

A dismaying technique through which the inadequacies of mental institutions are contained is the definition of the patient as "not appreciating anything better." Mental hospital staff members will say, "Why give them anything else, they'll just destroy it," in spite of the evidence of their eyes that most patients respond very well and "normally" to improved surroundings, taking great delight in new furniture and equipment. At the lay level this same technique shows up in the form of the belief, "They don't know what goes on around them anyway—it doesn't make the difference to them that it would to us."

The gross economic loss brought about by the methods of handling the mentally ill in North America may be intimately related to the expanding economy of the Western world. Countries like Norway* which seem to have made greater strides toward circumventing this loss can ill afford to sustain it. It is possible that as our economic frontiers shrink we will find ourselves impelled toward a more humane

---

* Norway, it is reported by Knudsen, has 49.1 per cent of its certified mentally ill persons living outside of mental hospitals. *International Journal of Social Psychiatry,* Vol. 1, No. 1.

handling of the mentally ill which will keep a great number of them from being lost forever in the giant state hospitals.

A most important question remains to be answered— "How do we, as members of society, deal psychologically with the loss of members to our community?"

Apparently we do this by assigning to the mentally ill a role which is close to the role of the dead. Many patients are discouraged from returning home, and others are forgotten as if they were dead once they have been in the hospital for any length of time. Personal communications from a number of hospital administrators have convinced us that many people remain in hospital as "institution cures" because they have nowhere to go.

In this section we have argued that there is a patterned way of reacting to mental illness in the larger society which we have called the pattern of denial, isolation, and insulation. We have listed some of the elements which we believe compose this pattern and examined their manifest and latent functions from the points of view of the greater community and of the mentally ill themselves. We have discussed some of the ways in which this pattern of values, beliefs, and behavior is articulated with other patterns in the social system and have touched on the problem of functional equivalents of the pattern. Later we will discuss the practical implications of the pattern, but now we will turn to the theoretical implications of this analysis, and we will suggest some hypotheses which may throw further light on this particular response to mental illness and on the more general problem of social control of deviance.

There are many unanswered questions embedded in this study. Even if the pattern were independently demonstrated and we were reasonably sure it was real, a multiplicity of information would obviously still be needed to establish what sorts of people are its chief carriers, what sorts deviate from it, and whether this deviance can be exploited to shift the pattern. At present we believe that certain evaluative orientations to life, as indicated by our "value variable," influence the way in which the pattern is acted out. We suspect that social class is important and also that the difference between "rigid" and "flexible" personalities may be important to consider when attempting to shift the pattern. The meaning of the pattern and its function will of course be unclear until further details are discovered.

Three serious questions can be raised as to the validity of the foregoing analysis. First, because the denial and isolation pattern of response to mental illness was not predicted before the exploratory field experiment, it must be expressed in hypothetical form. Only in this way will it be possible to demonstrate whether or not it has an actual existence; after all, it is possible to have a *post hoc* explanation which fits the facts without remainder but which is completely wrong. Certain primitive religions such as animism, in which all of life is successfully explained by a scientifically invalid principle, are cases in point. Second, the function of social integration which we imputed to the pattern must, like the pattern itself, be subjected to validation through the construction and testing of proper hypotheses. It is possible that it can be demonstrated that the pattern exists but that it has some other function than the one described here. Clearly it will be harder to demonstrate this function than to demonstrate the pattern, because it requires dealing with such concepts as "community solidarity" and "social disorganization," and hypotheses would have to take these illusive concepts into account. The third question concerns the validity of generalizing from the specific findings of this experiment, and therefore the related question of the nature of our experimental population.

Dealing with the third issue first, we will start with the assumption that our community, like all communities, was in some ways idiosyncratic owing to its particular history and development. We believe, however, that it is not unrepresentative of modern industrialized society. We believe this because of our own contact with the community, the observations of others such as Lipset,[49] and conversations with Dr. Shirley Star, who believes that Blackfoot respondents closely resemble American ones. Further, the St. Louis study[95] and a study in Trenton, New Jersey,[70] while both less intensive than our own, yield a similar patterning of results; in particular the St. Louis respondents showed a strong tendency to invoke what we would call the "normalizing" pattern in dealing with case histories.

It is our opinion that our experiment is as useful for the drawing of inferences as any single, localized study is likely to be, partly because our sample is reasonably representative of modern industrialized society, and partly because mental illness is a subject upon which attitudes are unlikely to have very marked regional differences.*

On the other hand, a specific limitation of this study resides in the failure to obtain complete coverage of the adult population of Blackfoot. We do not know the characteristics of the absent members, although we know that the age representation in the sample corresponds with that of the census. We do not know the sorts of people who failed to respond to our questionnaire the second time after having responded the first. We are unaware whether certain people who failed to respond the first time did respond the second.

The first and second questions raised above regarding the existence of the pattern described and the validity of imput-

---

* Dr. Star reports verbally that there is a slight tendency for illiterate Negro respondents to make use of magic when explaining mental illness, and this constitutes an exception.

ing to it, if it does exist, the functions described, are very important for the future of mental health education. We deliberately made our program representative of the type of educational program being used, in a less concentrated way, all over Canada and the United States.* Therefore it becomes doubly important to validate our findings. If we are using material and techniques which are less effective than they might be, then we must make this knowledge available to mental health workers. We must also make available to them any positive suggestions which we may be able to offer when more experimentation has either confirmed or denied our interpretation. In the next section we will discuss some of the practical things we discovered from our Blackfoot experience which might interest workers in this expanding and undoubtedly important field.

* There is no doubt that in certain large metropolitan centers service programs have been carried out in conjunction with mental health education. But for the great majority of people mental health education comes piecemeal and without the support of a new service.

Some Practical Suggestions

During our Blackfoot experiment in mental health education we gained through an intuitive process some practical
insights which have been helpful to us, and we would like
to present them here not as proven facts but as suggestions
arising from experience. First, however, we would like to
make clear what we mean by the term "mental health education." We are not here talking of it in the sense of education
directed at preventing mental illness in well people, nor in
the sense of education directed at fostering some ideal state
of "positive mental health," but rather in the sense of education about the nature of those already ill.

However, one of the fundamental working principles of
the mental health movement is to prevent mental illness.
This means that there must be some sort of working definition of mental health or else it becomes equated with absence
of mental illness and prevention becomes synonymous with
early treatment. Unfortunately, health—whether physical
or mental—is a very hard state to define and thus to foster,
and Smith's[80] excellent statement of the problem of definition

shows very clearly how complicated a concept "mental health" can be. On the other hand, mental illness is a recognized entity which is conceived as "preventable."

Partly because of the great difficulty in defining health without resorting to the concept of absence of illness, there has been a tendency for workers in the mental health field to select specific areas of endeavor which they have reason to hope will at worst prevent some illness and at best enhance mental health. For example, child guidance programs are undertaken in the belief that they will ultimately lower the incidence of mental illness, and perhaps enhance mental health, and rehabilitative schemes are undertaken explicitly to prevent the recurrence of mental illness and implicitly to strengthen individual resources and hence to improve mental health. We, in our program, were concerned with trying to add an increment of acceptance to the environment into which mental hospital patients return in the belief that this would lower the relapse rate among discharged patients.

In this chapter we are discussing a somewhat unsystematic collection of hunches which we acquired while doing this task. They are concerned with the method of entering a community and teaching its members somewhat strange facts and concepts and with the shifting of attitudes in general, whether in communities, friendship groups, working groups, families, or schools. We will introduce here examples from our more recent work which illustrate the successful use of some of these insights and hunches.

To begin chronologically, we believe that our method of entering Blackfoot was suitable to that community and was, in itself, successful. We also believe that the personal attributes and manner of the chief educator were equally suitable and successful.* We were very fortunate in this respect

* This point is made specifically because readers of this manuscript have raised this question.

because the community was very familiar to us, and we had no "foreignness" to overcome. If we had this job to do again we would begin it in much the same way, but we would try to create more continuity between the educators and the interviewing team in order to protect them from being targets for hostility—it will be recalled that the educators at no time experienced any hostility, nor did the interviewers until their second entrance. Above all we would try to prevent the masking by good interpersonal relations of any anxiety which the material being taught might be generating. In short, we would enter the town as we did, but we would ask ourselves whether smooth going was really an index of the degree to which difficult concepts were being accepted and learned, and above all we would have an independent evaluation of this process—a lack in the Blackfoot design.

Motivation toward learning seems to occur only under special circumstances. For example, when people do not feel that they have sufficient skill to reach a desirable goal, they are motivated to learn. An example from the mental hospital is relevant. While raising the standards of patient care in a state mental hospital, we were able through certain administrative changes to establish a group of new nursing positions for hospital aides. These positions were assigned high status and high pay, and tended to confer high prestige upon the incumbents. However, these incumbents, being new to the posts, were uncertain both about their new duties and about their own ability to carry them out. Because they wished to succeed in these new high-prestige roles, they were eager to learn new skills and to assimilate a new, and to them, strange point of view toward their patients. Unfortunately, it is not often possible to create motivation so conveniently, but it is possible in many situations to take advantage of fortuitous situations if the problem of motivation is kept in mind.

On the other hand, the mental hospital aides, even with extremely well-defined motivation, were, like the Blackfoot citizens, anxious and threatened when they were asked to change their attitudes. They differed from the Blackfoot people, however, in two ways: they were willing through their personal involvement with the educator to reveal this anxiety, and they were in a position to have this anxiety reduced in several ways. For one thing, these aides had been chosen for these positions by their peers, and so in a sense they had permission from their peers to adapt themselves to new ideas and to change their attitudes. Also by virtue of their special status and their common interest, they were a primary working group, and as such a group they had to develop work norms. Furthermore, as incumbents in new roles, they were allowed to demand information and to reject such of it as seemed too improbable to them. Finally, they did not have to accept any new idea until they could test it pragmatically. In all, their change of attitude was highly motivated and was supported by a protected environment so that they could have time to build equivalents for the functions their older attitudes had been performing for them.

Conditions similar to these may seem too difficult to duplicate in a community setting. However, they occur naturally from time to time, and in Blackfoot we were able, as we have said, to offer a study program to a group of young couples who were highly motivated toward being good parents. On the other hand, another opportunity to use available motivation escaped us. When we first entered the community, there was a fair degree of interest in the construction of a community recreation center. If this interest could have been increased to the point where temporarily, at any rate, it became of vital importance to the community, various organizations might have appointed people to a central committee responsible for bringing such a project to fruition. The members of this committee might then have felt a need for some help in planning their project. At this point a program which could make resources available to the committee members might have achieved a great deal. Different people might have been interested in the usefulness of such a centre for adolescent children, for older people, or even for the rehabilitation of the physically and mentally sick! Their interest might have led them to undertake limited pilot programs which could have been carried out by interested groups of citizens. With involvement in such programs, the members might have experienced a change in role, and perhaps a change in attitudes, because when roles change, the attitudes appropriate to the roles change, too. The educator at this point would have some chance to structure the new roles so that the shift in attitudes would be in the direction he desired.

When attitudes are changed through programs which are based on interaction among people interested in specific projects, it is specific attitudes which change. Thus attitudes toward colored people are changed when platoons are integrated, and attitudes toward the mentally ill are changed in planned and supervised interaction with the mentally ill. There may, however, be real dangers inherent in such specific piecemeal attitude changes. We do not know enough about the relationship within one person of his various attitudes—although Robin Williams[94] has given some very helpful suggestions about the possibility of undesirable side-effects being produced from random attempts. Furthermore, it seems probable that zeal for these specific changes, even when they are accomplished in a reasonably sophisticated way, may be in itself naive. Although we feel that our method of attempting change, namely to use all the materials available to us which were in common use among mental health educators, was a failure for all of the reasons we have gone into, we do not, on the other hand, believe that even if the method were properly refined, the whole assumption system which underlies such attempts would automatically be correct. On the contrary, we feel after our own experience that the whole ethic underlying the attempt to change the attitudes of others should be kept constantly in sight, and a general, coherent philosophy of both goals and acceptable methods should be worked out beforehand.

One of our errors in Blackfoot, and one which we have discussed extensively above, lay in our latent assumption that we knew the content of the Blackfoot people's attitudes toward human behavior and its causes. This assumption was never explicit, but became evident only when we analyzed our results. Later, when we worked with mental hospital aides, we were able to avoid this mistake and to work very effectively with a group of senior aides who were considered old and rigid and with unchangeably bad attitudes. In this case we consciously analyzed these attitudes, and looked carefully for the relationship between those considered "bad" and the situation in which the men found themselves. As a result, we were able to plan much more precisely what the area of change had to be. In other words, we gave attention to the function which these attitudes had for those who held them. It was often necessary to alter the situation so that the function of the attitude disappeared before it could be given up.

While program planners often give a good deal of thought to the personality of their educators, the effect of the educator's role should also be taken into consideration. It is probable that a psychiatrist—as in our case—should not be placed in a position where he is the chief organizer and one of the major contributors to a mental health program. Such activity, to most people, is simply not appropriate to the role of a specialist physician, and this probably acted against acceptance of our program in Blackfoot. If a psychiatrist has a clinical role in a community program, he can successfully assume a secondary role as an educator, but to give him a primary task so far removed from that customarily expected of him must give a decided impression of deviance. By contrast, in the hospital education program which we have mentioned above, the psychiatrist was an entirely appropriate educator because the relationship of the education program and the treatment of patients was immediately evident, and because doctors are expected to instruct hospital personnel.

Consideration of appropriate educators raises the question of involving local people in such a program and of the best method of communicating to them the special information they need. We did not attempt to use local people as educators in Blackfoot, but it was our impression during our later hospital experiment, where we used hospital aides to educate those under them, that once the senior aides had internalized the body of knowledge which we wished to teach them, they could communicate it to their peers more effectively than we could. This experience suggests the advisability of working with a small group in a definite and circumscribed community program and letting the members interpret the project and its meaning to the remainder of the community. In Blackfoot the program item which we subjectively judged the most successful—although this may reflect the values of the investigators—was the involvement of the Legion members in a hospital visiting program. Unfortunately this was not possible until late in the program, owing to conditions in the hospital, and we did not realize until too late the leverage which this type of activity might give us in the community. We realize that women are active in volunteer roles in large hospitals, but we recommend the more extensive involvement of groups of men in the problems of the large hospital as well as in rehabilitation programs. This type of activity among community leaders may well lead to a gradual replacement of the isolation response to mental illness with a more integrative type of response which, while more functional for the mentally ill, still does not threaten the underpinnings of the social order.

Turning away now from the problems inherent in community programs, we would like to make a partial and incomplete listing of some of the practical ideas about the general area of attitude change which we learned when dwelling upon our Blackfoot experience. First, a partial insight into effective educational methods is provided by responses to the cases described in the intensive interview. It will be remembered that the description of a delinquent child drew remarks much closer to the ideas of the interviewers themselves than did any of the other cases. Modern teaching about child development and training has really "taken" and become a significant part of people's thinking. The brisk sale of books on this subject and its popularity for discussion at parents' groups further indicate its acceptability. Perhaps the isolation of today's small family from grandparents has created a need among young mothers for advice about raising children. The abundance of literature, lectures, and films about how to bring up children seems to be filling a gap left by the outdating of the methods used by past generations. However, we do not know in what precise way this change of attitude has come about, and a retrospective study of how attitudes toward the deviance of children came to be so different from attitudes toward deviant adults seems of paramount importance. Also, we do not know how people are able to keep their permissive and psychologically oriented attitudes toward deviant children separate from their more judgmental and normatively oriented attitudes toward deviant adults. Our own analysis gives a partial explanation, but there is a very practical need for an intensive study of individuals and their separate ways of handling this problem. Finally, we do not know why the same group of people who give child-oriented responses to the story of a deviant child give responses which do not seem child-oriented at all when they are asked, "What kind of child is liked in this community?" We suggest that those who are familiar with the sociology, history, and psychology of modern child-raising practices can make a most important practical contribution to the understanding of shifts in attitudes about vital interpersonal matters.

Probably our most important practical insight was that it is impossible to think too hard *before* such an experiment. Specifically our own best ideas about how to teach hospital aides arose, at least in part, from the functional analysis we made of our failure, by any objective measure, to change attitudes in Blackfoot. Had we had a more comprehensive theoretical framework before we entered Blackfoot, we might have been able to predict that we would raise anxiety and hostility while attitudes remained unchanged if we used intensively the materials then popular for many different kinds of "mental health education." If we had been able to predict this, we would have had a much firmer finding, and we could state categorically some things which we have put forward here conjecturally, for prediction is the earmark of science. We would have painted a clear and intelligible stroke instead of a crude one upon an almost empty canvas. In short, our most important *practical* insight has been that there is nothing so practical as a *good theory*.

Bibliography

1. Aberle, D. F., "Introducing Preventive Psychiatry into a Community," *Human Organization,* IX, 1950, pp. 5–9.
2. Adland, B., *Attitudes of Eastern European Jews Toward Mental Illness,* Smith College Studies in Social Work, Vol. 8, 1937.
3. Adorno, T. W., Frenkel-Brunswik, E., Levinson, D. J., and Sanford, R. N., *The Authoritarian Personality.* N.Y., Harper, 1950.
4. Allport, Gordon, "Prejudice, a Problem in Psychological and Social Causation," in *Toward a General Theory of Action.* Cambridge, Mass., Harvard University Press, 1951.
5. Bales, R. Freed, "Types of Social Structure as Factors in 'Cures' for Alcohol Addiction," *Applied Anthropology,* I, No. 3, 1942, pp. 1–13.
6. Barber, Bernard, Apathy (unpublished Ph.D. thesis), Harvard University, 1952.
7. Barton, Walter, Address to Boston Society for Applied Anthropology, March, 1954.
8. Beers, C., "Epilogue, the Mental Hygiene Movement" in *A Mind That Found Itself,* 9th Ed. N.Y., Doubleday and Co., 1953.

9. Belknap, I., and Friedaam, H. J., "Age and Sex Categories as Sociological Variables in the Mental Disorders of Later Maturity," *Am. Sociol. Rev.*, XIV, 1949, pp. 367–376.

10. Bell, Norman, Family Reactions to Strain (unpublished M.A. thesis), University of Toronto, 1953.

11. Bleuler, E. P., *Dementia Praecox or the Group of Schizophrenias.* N.Y., International University Press, 1950.

12. Burrow, T., "Insanity, a Social Problem," *Am. J. Sociol.*, 32, July, 1926, pp. 80–87.

13. Cameron, D. E., "The *Day Hospital,* An Experimental Form of Hospitalization for Psychiatric Patients," *Mod. Hosp.*, Vol. 69, No. 3, September, 1947, pp. 60–62.

14. Caudill, W., Redlich, F. C., Gilmore, H. R., and Brody, E. B., "Social Structure and Interaction Processes on a Psychiatric Ward," *Am. J. Orthopsychiat.*, XXII, April, 1952, pp. 314–34.

15. Caudill, W., and Stainbrook, E., "Some Covert Effects of Communication Difficulties in a Psychiatric Ward," paper read at 109th Annual Meeting of the American Psychiatric Association, May, 1953.

16. Crutcher, Hester B., *Foster Home Care for Mental Patients.* N.Y., The Commonwealth Fund, 1944.

17. Davis, Kingsley, "Mental Hygiene and the Class Structure," *Psychiatry,* I, 1938, pp. 55–65.

18. Davis, Kingsley, "The Application of Science to Personal Relations," *Am. Sociol. Rev.,* April, 1936, pp. 236–247.

19. Deutsch, Albert, *The Shame of the States.* N.Y., Harcourt, 1948.

20. Deutsch, Albert, *The Mentally Ill in America,* 2nd Ed. N.Y., Columbia University Press, 1949.

21. Deutsch, Albert, "Recent Trends in Mental Hospital Care," National Conference of Social Work, *Social Work in the Current Scene* (Selected Papers, 77, Conference of Social Work.) N.Y., Columbia University Press, 1950.

22. Deutsch, M., and Collins, M. E., *Interracial Housing: A Psychological Evaluation of a Social Experiment.* Minneapolis, University of Minnesota Press, 1951.

23. Dollard, John, "The Psychotic Person Seen Culturally," *Am. J. Sociol.,* XXXIX, 1934, pp. 637–48.

24. Dunham, H. Warren, "The Current Status of Ecological Research in Mental Disorder," *Social Forces,* XXV, March, 1947, pp. 321–26.

25. Durkheim, Emile, *The Division of Labor in Society.* Glencoe, Ill., The Free Press, 1947.

26. Durkheim, Emile, *Suicide.* Glencoe, Ill., The Free Press, 1951.

27. Eaton, J. W., "The Assessment of Mental Health," *Am. J. Psychiat.,* CVIII, August, 1951, pp. 81–90.

28. Faris, R. E. L., "Cultural Isolation and the Schizophrenic Personality," *Am. J. Sociol.,* XL, 1934, pp. 155–64.

29. Faris, R. and Dunham, W., *Mental Disorders in Urban Areas.* Chicago, University of Chicago Press, 1939.

30. Faris, R. E. L., "Ecological Factors in Human Behavior," in Hunt, J. McV. (ed.), *Personality and Behavior Disorders,* II. N.Y., Ronald Press, 1947.

31. Felix, R. H., "Mental Hygiene as Public Health Practice," *Am. J. Orthopsychiat.,* Vol. XXI, No. 3, October, 1951, pp. 707–16.

32. Felix, R. H., and Kramer, M., "Research in the Epidemiology of Mental Illness," *Pub. Health Rep.,* LXVII, February, 1952, pp. 152–60.

33. Fox, Renee Claire, Ward F-Second and the Research Physician; A Study in Stress and Ways of Coming to Terms with Stress (unpublished manuscript), Department of Social Relations, Harvard University, 1952.

34. Freud, S., "Psychoanalytic Notes upon an Autobiographical Account of a Case of Paranoia," in *Collected Papers,* III. London, Hogarth Press, 1925, p. 387.

35. Gerard, Donald L., and Seigel, Joseph, "The Family Background of Schizophrenia," *Psychiatric Quart.,* XXIV, January, 1950, pp. 47–73.

36. Gilbert, Doris, Ideologies Concerning Mental Illness (unpublished Ph.D. thesis), Harvard University, 1954.

37. Halliday, James L., *Psychosocial Medicine.* N.Y., Norton, 1948.

38. Hollingshead, A. B., and Redlich, F. C., "Social Class and Psychiatric Disorders," in *Interrelations Between the Social Environment and Psychiatric Disorders.* N.Y., Milbank Memorial Fund, 1953.

39. Hollingshead, A. B., and Redlich, F. C., "Schizophrenia and Social Structure," *Am. J. Psychiat.*, CX, No. 9, March, 1954, pp. 695–701.

40. Homans, G. C., "Group Factors in Worker Productivity," in *Fatigue of Workers, Its Relation to Industrial Production*. N.Y., Reinhold, 1941.

40a. Howe, Louisa P., in *Community Programs for Mental Health* (ed. Kotinsky and Witmer). Cambridge, Mass., Harvard University Press, 1955.

41. Hyman, Herbert H., "The Value System of Different Classes, A Social Psychological Contribution to the Analysis of Stratification," in Bendix, R., and Lipset, S. M., *Class, Status and Power*. Glencoe, Ill., The Free Press, 1953.

42. Jahoda, Marie, "Toward a Social Psychology of Mental Health," in Rose, Arnold M., *Mental Health and Mental Disorder*. N.Y., Norton, 1955.

43. Kilgour, A. J., "Colony Gheel," *Am. J. Psychiat.*, XCII, 1936, pp. 3–6.

44. Kinsey, A. C., Pomeroy, W. B., and Martin, C. E., *Sexual Behavior in the Human Male*. Philadelphia, Saunders, 1948.

45. Kluckhohn, Clyde, *Navajo Witchcraft*, Papers of the Peabody Museum, XXII, No. 2, p. 47a. Cambridge, Mass., The Museum, Harvard University, 1944.

46. Lemert, E. M., *Social Pathology*. N.Y., McGraw-Hill, 1951.

47. Lemert, Edwin, "Legal Commitment and Social Control," *Sociology and Social Research*, May–June, 1946, pp. 370–78.

48. Lewin, K., "Group Decision and Social Change," in *Readings in Social Psychology* (ed. Swanson, Newcombe, and Hartley). N.Y., Henry Holt, 1952.

49. Lipset, S. M., *Agrarian Socialism*. Berkeley, Calif., University of California Press, 1950.

50. Martin, M. G., "A Practical Treatment Program for a Mental Hospital 'Back' Ward," *Am. J. Psychiat.*, CVI, No. 10, April, 1950, pp. 758–60.

51. McNemar, Q., "Opinion-Attitude Methodology," *Psychological Bulletin*, XLIII, July, 1946, pp. 289–374.

52. Merton, R. K., "Manifest and Latent Functions," in *Social Theory and Social Structure*. Glencoe, Ill., The Free Press, 1949.

53. Merton, R. K., *Mass Persuasion*. N.Y., Harper, 1946.

54. Merton, R. K., "The Social Structure and Anomie," in *Social Theory and Social Structure*. Glencoe, Ill., The Free Press, 1951.

55. *Mental Health in Virginia*. Richmond, Virginia Department of Mental Hygiene and Hospitals, 1953.

56. *Mental Hygiene Fact Book No. 57*. Trenton, N.J., Department of Agencies and Institutions, 1952.

57. Milbank Memorial Fund, *Epidemiology of Mental Disorder*. N.Y., Milbank Memorial Fund, 1950.

58. Mills, C. W., "The Professional Ideology of Social Pathologists," *Am. J. Sociol.*, XLIX, No. 2, 1943, pp. 165–80.

59. Northrop, F. C., *The Meeting of East and West*. N.Y., Macmillan, 1946.

60. Parsons, T., *The Social System*. Glencoe, Ill., The Free Press, 1950.

61. Parsons, T., "Illness and the Role of the Physician: A Sociological Perspective," *Am. J. Orthopsychiat.*, XXI, July, 1951, pp. 452–60.

62. Parsons, T., Bales, R. F., and Shils, E., *Working Papers in the Theory of Action*. Glencoe, Ill., The Free Press, 1953.

63. Parsons, T., and Shils, E. A. (eds.), *Toward a General Theory of Action*. Cambridge, Mass., Harvard University Press, 1951.

64. Parsons, T., and Fox, R., "Illness, Therapy and the Modern Urban American Family," *J. Social Issues,* VIII, No. 4, 1952, pp. 31–44.

65. Pearse, I. H., and Crocker, L. H., *The Peckham Experiment*. London, Allen and Unwin, 1943.

66. Paul, B. D., "Mental Disorder and Self-Regulating Processes in Culture: A Guatemalan Illustration," in *Interrelations Between the Social Environment and Psychiatric Disorders*. N.Y., Milbank Memorial Fund, 1953.

67. Pollock, Horatio M., "A Brief History of Family Care of Mental Patients in America," *Am. J. Psychiat.*, CII, 1945, pp. 351–61.

68. Proehl, E. A., "The Transition from Institutional to Social Adjustment," *Am. Sociol. Rev.,* III, No. 4, August, 1938, pp. 534–40.

69. Ramsey, G. V., and Seipp, M., "Public Opinions and Information Concerning Mental Health," *J. Clin. Psych.,* IV, No. 4, October, 1948, pp. 397–406.

70. Ramsey, G. V., and Seipp, M., "Attitudes and Opinions Concerning Mental Illness," *Psychiatric Quart.,* XXII, July, 1948, pp. 428–44.

71. Redlich, F. C., "What the Citizen Knows About Psychiatry," *Ment. Hyg.,* XXXIV, January, 1950, pp. 64–79.

72. Rose, A., *Studies in the Reduction of Prejudices.* Chicago, American Council on Race Relations, 1947.

73. Rowland, H., "Interaction Process in the State Mental Hospital," *Psychiatry,* I, No. 3, August, 1938, pp. 323–37.

74. Rowland, H., "Friendship Patterns in the State Mental Hospitals," *Psychiatry,* II, 1939, pp. 363–73.

75. Ruesch, Jurgen, and Bateson, Gregory, *Communication—The Social Matrix of Psychiatry.* N.Y., Norton, 1951.

76. Schneider, David M., "The Social Dynamics of Physical Disability in Army Basic Training," *Psychiatry,* X, August, 1947, pp. 323–33.

77. Schwartz, Charlotte G., "The Rehabilitation of Mental Hospital Patients" (mimeographed bibliography). Washington, D.C., National Institute of Mental Health, 1952.

78. Schwartz, Charlotte G., *Analysis of the Literature on the Rehabilitation of Mental Hospital Patients* (mimeographed). Washington, D.C., National Institute of Mental Health, December, 1952.

79. Slotkin, J. S., "Nature and Effects of Social Interaction in Schizophrenia," *J. Abnorm. & Social Psychol.,* XXXVII, July, 1942, pp. 345–68.

80. Smith, M. Brewster, "Optima of Mental Health," *Psychiatry,* XIII, 1950, pp. 503–10.

81. Stanton, A. H., and Schwartz, M. S., "A Social Psychological Study of Incontinence," *Psychiatry,* XIII, 1950, pp. 399–416.

82. Stanton, A. H., "Psychiatric Theory and Institutional Context,' *Psychiatry,* XVII, No. 1, 1954, pp. 19–26.

83. Stanton, A. H., and Schwartz, M. S., *The Mental Hospital.* N.Y., Basic Books, 1954.

84. Stevenson, George S., "Dynamic Considerations in Community Functions," *Mental Hygiene,* Vol. XXXIV, No. 4, October, 1950, pp. 531–546.

85. Stouffer, S., et al. (*a*), *The American Soldier,* Vol. II. Princeton University Press, 1950.

86. Stouffer, S., et al. (*b*), *Measurement and Prediction.* Princeton University Press, 1950.

87. Sullivan, H. S., "Socio-Psychiatric Research—Its Implications for the Schizophrenia Problem and for Mental Hygiene," *Am. J. Psychiat.,* Vol. 87, No. 6, 1931, pp. 977–92.

88. Sullivan, H. S., *The Interpersonal Theory of Psychiatry.* N.Y., Norton, 1953.

89. Tietze, C., Lemkau, P., and Cooper, M., "Schizophrenia, Manic-Depressive Psychosis and Social-economic Status," *Am. J. Sociol.,* XLVII, 1941, pp. 167–75.

90. Tudor, G. E., "A Sociopsychiatric Nursing Approach to Intervention in a Problem of Mutual Withdrawal on a Mental Hospital Ward," *Psychiatry,* XV, No. 2, 1952, pp. 193–217.

91. Useem, J., Tangent, P., and Useem, R., "Stratification in Prairie Town," *Am. Sociol. Rev.,* June, 1942.

92. Warner, J., "The Society, the Individual and His Mental Disorders," *Am. J. Psychol.,* September, 1937.

93. Weinberg, S. Kirson, *Society and Personality Disorders.* N.Y., Prentice-Hall, 1952.

94. Williams, Robin, *The Reduction of Intergroup Tensions.* N.Y., Social Science Research Council, *Bull.,* 57, 1947.

95. Woodward, Julian L., "Changing Ideas on Mental Illness and Its Treatment," *Am. Sociol. Rev.,* XVI, No. 4, August, 1951, pp. 443–54.

The Natural History
of the Scales

A. *The Likert Scale*

The first research instrument with which we worked was designed to measure a quality of "constructiveness versus non-constructiveness" in attitudes toward mental illness and consisted of the following 28-item Likert-type scale. We are grateful to Mr. Neil Agnew of the Department of Health, Saskatchewan, for allowing us to use this scale, which he developed.

1. There are a few exceptions, but generally mental hospital patients are pretty much alike.

2. If I were employed at a job I wouldn't hesitate to share my office with someone who had been mentally ill.

3. It would be wise to discourage former mental hospital patients from entering the Province, since they are likely to become an expense.

4. I would be willing to work in a mental hospital.

5. We should strongly discourage our children from marrying anyone who has been mentally ill.

6. I would be willing to trust someone who had been mentally ill with financial matters.

7. Those who live in communities from which mentally sick people come ought to be considered partially responsible for their breakdown.

8. It would be wise to stay as far away as possible from former mental hospital patients.

9. If I owned an empty lot beside my house I would be willing to sell it to a former mental hospital patient.

10. I wouldn't work for anyone who had been mentally ill.

11. The family and friends of a mentally sick person ought to be considered to need mental health guidance.

12. I would try to keep it a secret if one of my family became mentally ill.

13. The police should make periodic check-ups on former mental hospital patients.

14. Training in the principles of mental health is much more important than training in the three "R's."

15. All of us show symptoms of mental illness at one time or another.

16. If I were resident owner of an apartment house I would hesitate to rent living quarters to a former mental hospital patient.

17. Sex deviates should be severely punished.

18. I would be willing to take training which would make me eligible to sponsor a mental hospital patient when he was discharged.

19. Mentally ill people should be considered as weak-willed.

20. If I were a personnel manager I would be willing to hire a former mental hospital patient.

21. It would not be wise to bring up your family in a town in which a mental hospital was located.

22. I would marry a member of a family in which there is mental illness.

23. We should take pity on people who have been mentally ill.

24. Those who live in communities from which mentally sick people come should be considered to need mental health guidance.

25. It would be unwise to encourage the close friendship of a person who has been mentally ill.

26. I would be willing to room with a former mental hospital patient.

27. I would never trust anyone who had been mentally ill with my children.

28. I can imagine myself becoming mentally ill.

Responses to the items of this scale were divided into six levels of intensity, varying from "strongly agree" to "strongly disagree," the total possible score being 140 points, with responses scored from 0 to 5.

The scale discriminated among psychiatrists, graduate nurses, and student nurses when the means and standard deviations of the scores made by the members of these groups were compared with a t-test. We thought, therefore, that it would be possible to pre-test the scale for our own uses by measuring any change in the attitudes of a group of student nurses over the two-month period of their training. Accordingly a series of 50 student nurses was chosen for study. The scale was administered at the beginning of their affiliation in a psychiatric hospital and again at the conclusion, two months later. When the average score "before" was compared (t-test) with the average score "after," it was found to be significantly higher.

An examination of the content of the scale, however, led us to the belief that many of the nurses were responding to it differently from one another because of personality differences rather than because of the content of the items. Therefore, we interviewed 20 nurses and found that many, judged on the basis of our conversations to hold much the same attitudes, had scored quite differently because some preferred to express strong agreement or disagreement while others preferred to express mild agreement or disagreement. It was our conclusion from these interviews that differences in score were at least partly generated by differences in the personalities of the respondents. It was our general impression that the more shy and withdrawn girls tended to make middle-range scores because of their dislike of underlining the more extreme alternative answers. By the same token, the more outspoken girls with overtly hostile tendencies scored higher or lower. It was possible in the limiting case for two girls to have chosen all the "constructive" answers and still to differ by 56 points because of different intensities of response. All in all it appeared that dichotomized answers might be more useful to us.

Further examination of the results of the trial measurement showed that certain items were consistently drawing agreement from all the nurses and were therefore acting only as "padding" items.

B. *The Guttman Scales*

These two defects in the scale led us to the conclusion that a general overhauling of the questionnaire was needed. In consultation with Dr. Star of the National Opinion Research Center, we decided to attempt to scale the items according to Guttman's[86] method, feeling that it would be valuable to know whether or not we were tapping a unidimensional attitude. Because the questionnaire items completely failed to scale with the six levels of intensity retained in the responses our decision to dichotomize the responses was reinforced. A second attempt was made to produce a unidimensional scale. This time we found 10 "easy" items which were being responded to positively by more than 80 per cent of respondents. (Although some items were expressed negatively, and "disagree" was the response which earned the score, all responses for which a score is given are called "positive.")

Items with higher than 80 per cent positive responses fail to discriminate well between respondents, and they reduce errors in the scale artificially to a maximum of 20 per cent. When these "easy" items were removed we had two bodies of items which each scaled as units but which did not scale together. Upon examining these groups of items, we realized that we were dealing with two different sets of content, one apparently concerned with social distance from the mentally ill and the other related to the degree of "responsibility" which the respondent felt he would accept for mental illness. The content of the items suggests that these problems are seen to be continuous between the greater social system and the small face-to-face group. The items in the following scale, it is immediately apparent, run from acceptance of responsibility for mental illness occurring in the nuclear family to acceptance of responsibility for mental illness occurring in the community. However, the meaning of the term *responsibility* raises some very difficult questions.

When the items were taken from the Likert scale and revamped for the Guttman scale, it was assumed that "responsibility" referred to causation. The latent assumption was that mental illness arose in interaction, and that therefore the people with whom most interaction occurred—and who therefore had the deepest relationship—would be "responsible" in the sense of having provided an environment which was related causally to the breakdown. At no time was it assumed that there was a conscious causation, let alone a motivated one! In short, mental illness was viewed by the investigators as well as the educators as being primarily a response to environment and only secondarily emergent or biological. It is, however, uncertain whether the respondents assigned this meaning to the items, and we will return to this point shortly.

SOCIAL DISTANCE SCALE

1. We should strongly discourage our children from marrying anyone who has been mentally ill.

2. I would marry a member of a family in which there is mental illness.

3. I would be willing to trust someone who had been mentally ill with financial matters.

4. I would be willing to room with a former mental hospital patient.

5. If I were resident owner of an apartment house I would hesitate to rent living quarters to a former mental hospital patient.

6. If I were employed at a job I wouldn't hesitate to share my office with someone who had been mentally ill.

(*Reproducibility*—90.0)

SOCIAL RESPONSIBILITY SCALE

1. Those who live in communities from which mentally sick people come should be considered to need mental health guidance.

2. Those who live in communities from which mentally sick people come ought to be considered partially responsible for their breakdown.

3. The family and friends of a mentally sick person ought to be considered to need mental health guidance.

4. I can imagine myself becoming mentally ill.

5. I would be willing to take training which would make me eligible to sponsor a mental hospital patient when he was discharged.

(*Reproducibility*—88.8)

Because the scales were short, we interdigitated new items which seemed to belong logically in the series, and because of the homogeneity of the nursing population used for pre-test, we arranged to test the new instrument with an entirely different group. A population of civil servants was selected which was excessively weighted with clerical workers and professionals and had too few manual workers but was more varied than the nurses had been.

One hundred and twenty-four completed questionnaires were obtained, and rescaling yielded the following 9 useable Distance Scale items and 8 useable Responsibility Scale items.

SOCIAL DISTANCE SCALE (VERSION 2)

1. I would be willing to room with a former mental hospital patient.

2. I would marry a member of a family in which there is mental illness.

3. We should strongly discourage our children from marrying anyone who has been mentally ill.

4. I would be willing to trust someone who had been mentally ill with financial matters.

5. I would never trust anyone who had been mentally ill with my children.

6. If I were resident owner of an apartment house I would hesitate to rent living quarters to a former mental hospital patient.

7. I would be willing to sponsor a person who had been mentally ill for membership in my favorite club or society.

8. If I were employed at a job I wouldn't hesitate to share my office with someone who had been mentally ill.

9. If I owned an empty lot beside my house I would be willing to sell it to a former mental hospital patient.

(*Reproducibility—*89.5)

SOCIAL RESPONSIBILITY SCALE (VERSION 2)

1. Those who live in communities from which mentally sick people come ought to be considered partially responsible for their breakdown.

2. Those who live in communities from which mentally sick people come should be considered to need mental health guidance.

3. The family and friends of a mentally sick person ought to be considered to need mental health guidance.

4. I would feel no personal responsibility if a member of my favorite club or society became mentally ill.

5. I would feel partially responsible if a member of my family had a serious mental breakdown.

6. I would be willing to take training which would make me eligible to sponsor a mental hospital patient when he was discharged.

7. In spite of our best efforts there is very little which we can do to prevent mental illness.

8. It would be wise to discourage former mental hospital patients from entering our community since they are likely to become an expense.

(*Reproducibility—*89.9)

It is of some peripheral interest that of all the populations measured it was among this group of civil servants that the largest number of responsibility items scaled. The responsibility theme did not constitute such a long continuum for any previous or subsequent group tested; and this fact suggested that this group saw a general "responsibility" element in items which did not have this meaning for others. It is obvious that no scale item can be quite freed of secondary or alternative meaning, and this secondary meaning may be selected as the primary focus of the question. In limiting cases, a statement such as "I feel responsibility for mental illness" removes the conflicting minor theme, but the idea of building a scale with such statements by simply inserting the words "much," "a great deal," etc., before the word "responsibility" is clearly absurd. Our civil servant population seemed able to focus on the theme of responsibility for mental illness, keeping the secondary themes (of clubs, communities, kinship ties, etc.) out of focus far more successfully than any other group tested.

In this trial we again lost items because of excess numbers of positive responses, and some items, previously scaleable with the nurses, failed to scale with the civil servants. For example, the item "I would be willing to work in a mental hospital," previously successful, failed to scale. Analysis showed the positive responses to this item to be distributed at the top and bottom of the scale; both high- and low-scoring people answered "yes," while those with middle-range scores answered "no." Perhaps the secondary theme of "occupation" is dominant in this item for low-scoring people, and they are indicating not their attitude toward mental illness but their attitude toward jobs.

Although some items had been discarded from the scale because too many nurses had responded to them positively, it was reasoned that nurses are a special group who have an institutionalized set of humanitarian values and norms about sickness, and that they might therefore be expected to be highly accepting of people defined as ill. In order not to waste items that might be useful in a lay population we reinserted all the original items which had been dropped from the series because of 80 per cent or more successful responses. This concluded our primary manipulations, and we took the following twenty-three-item questionnaire into the field. From it the final scales, used throughout the analysis, were selected by the Guttman technique:

1. I would be willing to trust someone who had been mentally ill with financial matters.

2. Our community should not be expected to take the responsibility of providing suitable jobs for its former mental hospital patients.

3. Those who live in communities from which mentally sick people come ought to be considered partially responsible for their breakdown.

4. If I were resident owner of an apartment house I would hesitate to rent living quarters to a former mental hospital patient.

5. If I were employed at a job I *wouldn't* hesitate to share my office with someone who had been mentally ill.

6. I *wouldn't* work for anyone who had been mentally ill.

7. I would marry a member of a family in which there is mental illness.

8. I would never trust anyone who had been mentally ill with my children.

9. The family and friends of a mentally sick person ought to be considered to need mental health guidance.

10. I would *not* lend money to a person who had been mentally ill.

11. I would be willing to room with a former mental hospital patient.

12. It would be wise to discourage former mental hospital patients from entering our community since they are likely to become an expense.

13. I would be willing to take training which would make me eligible to sponsor a mental hospital patient when he was discharged.

14. I would feel no personal responsibility if a member of my favorite club or society became mentally ill.

15. Those who live in communities from which mentally sick people come should be considered to need mental health guidance.

16. In spite of our best efforts there is very little we can do to prevent mental illness.

17. I can imagine myself becoming mentally ill.

18. I would feel partially responsible if a member of my family had a serious mental breakdown.

19. I would be willing to sponsor a person who had been mentally ill for membership in my favorite club or society.

20. We should strongly discourage our children from marrying anyone who has been mentally ill.

21. If I owned an empty lot beside my house I would be willing to sell it to a former mental hospital patient.

22. Only professionally trained people such as doctors or ministers should feel responsibility for other people's problems of mental health and mental illness.

23. I can imagine myself falling in love with a person who had been mentally ill.

All the items from the Distance and Responsibility series which had been in the first questionnaire were included in the resurvey questionnaire whether or not they had scaled. In addition we added two new

Responsibility items designed to fall logically between those dealing with responsibility at the community level and those dealing with it at the close kinship level (items 9 and 18 below):

1. If I were employed at a job I wouldn't hesitate to share my office with someone who had been mentally ill.

2. Those who live in communities from which mentally sick people come ought to be considered partially responsible for their breakdown.

3. If I were resident owner of an apartment house I would hesitate to rent living quarters to a former mental hospital patient.

4. The personal friends of a mentally ill person ought to be considered partly responsible for his breakdown.

5. I wouldn't work for anyone who had been mentally ill.

6. I feel that all those who take part in a child's training in early life should feel partially responsible for mental illness which develops at a later age.

7. I would be willing to sponsor a person who had been mentally ill for membership in my favorite club or society.

8. I would be willing to room with a former mental hospital patient.

9. I would feel partially responsible if a person who worked for me became mentally ill.

10. Those who live in communities from which mentally sick people come should be considered to need mental health guidance.

11. We should strongly discourage our children from marrying anyone who has been mentally ill.

12. If I owned an empty lot beside my house I would be willing to sell it to a former mental hospital patient.

13. All those who participate in child training are in need of mental health guidance.

14. I would feel partially responsible if a member of my family had a serious mental breakdown.

15. Good community recreation facilities would lessen the amount of mental illness in a community.

16. I can imagine myself falling in love with a person who had been mentally ill.

17. The family and friends of a mentally sick person ought to be considered partly responsible if he becomes mentally ill.

18. The people with whom a person works on his job ought to be considered partly responsible if he becomes mentally ill.

Upon rescaling the items again by Guttman's method, it was found that the two new ones fitted satisfactorily into a continuum in both communities with the following scale emerging (reproducibility in Blackfoot was 91.8 per cent and in Deerville 91.3 per cent) :

1. Those who live in communities from which mentally sick people come ought to be considered partially responsible for their breakdown.
2. The people with whom a person works on his job ought to be considered partly responsible if he becomes mentally ill.
3. I would feel partially responsible if a person who worked for me became mentally ill.
4. Those who live in communities from which mentally sick people come should be considered to need mental health guidance.
5. The family and friends of a mentally sick person ought to be considered to need mental health guidance.
6. I would feel partially responsible if a member of my family had a serious mental breakdown.

The order of the foregoing scale items suggests that the presence of the word "responsibility" makes the question difficult to respond to positively except where it refers to one's immediate family, whereas the use of the phrase "mental health guidance" seems to make the item relatively easy to agree with. On the other hand, the type of relationship described in the item seems important in determining the number of positive responses.

Again the question of the meaning of the word "responsibility" crops up. It would seem logical that the meaning taken is that intended, namely responsibility for causation. When one considers that of the four items containing the word "responsibility" the two concerned with employer-employee relationships were easier to answer than the one community question and harder to answer than the one family-and-friends question, it seems reasonable that the meaning assigned is "responsibility for cause," because a business relationship lies between a friendship relationship and a community relationship. The results are unreasonable if the meaning is "responsibility for care," because both families and communities undertake this responsibility, while business associates do not.

On the other hand, there is evidence from two sources that at least some of our respondents did use the alternative meaning of this word. First, a small group of professional people were asked what meaning they assigned and they all agreed to responsibility for *care*. However, this group, besides being selectedly professional, were not exposed to the original format of the questionnaire but were asked one or two questions orally. We are inclined to think on the balance of evidence that most respondents were in some way influenced by this format to take the intended meaning of "responsibility for cause" from the items. A second source of doubt, however, is the distribution of errors in the Guttman scale. There is a tendency for error to be caused by some people responding to the item containing the word *responsibility* differently from the "mental health guidance" items and this would suggest a tendency to split the meaning of the scale. Our best judgment at this time is that *most* respondents were responding to a more general concept of responsibility* than any of the items specifically indicates— otherwise there would not have been a scale at all†—but that some respondents did answer each question at a more concrete and specific level and of these, some assigned the meaning "responsibility for care" while others assigned the meaning "responsibility for cause."

The Distance items, without new additions, rescaled with reproducibilities of 90.1 per cent in Deerville and 91.1 per cent in Blackfoot.

RESURVEY—DEERVILLE
DISTANCE SCALE

1. We should strongly discourage our children from marrying anyone who has been mentally ill.

2. I can imagine myself falling in love with a person who had been mentally ill.

3. I would be willing to room with a former mental hospital patient.

4. If I were resident owner of an apartment house I would hesitate to rent living quarters to a former mental hospital patient.

5. I *wouldn't* work for anyone who had been mentally ill.

---

* See also p. 179 for discussion of lost items.

† It has been suggested that the scaling property of the Responsibility Scale is an artifact arising from the secondary meaning in the scale (that is, degree of relationship, or social distance). This explanation would solve the problem of the meaning of the scale but probably is incorrect, although it appeals strongly to reason. The trouble is that *if* the scaling property was caused by the social distance element in the items, then the items should form one scale with the Distance Scale. Further, if they were of a mildly different order of distance, they most certainly should correlate with the Distance items, and this they do not.

6. If I owned an empty lot beside my house I would be willing to sell it to a former mental hospital patient.

7. I would be willing to sponsor a person who had been mentally ill for membership in my favorite club or society.

RESURVEY—BLACKFOOT
DISTANCE SCALE

1. We should strongly discourage our children from marrying anyone who has been mentally ill.

2. I can imagine myself falling in love with a person who had been mentally ill.

3. I would be willing to room with a former mental hospital patient.

4. If I owned an empty lot beside my house I would be willing to sell it to a former mental hospital patient.

5. I would be willing to sponsor a person who had been mentally ill for membership in my favorite club or society.

6. If I were employed at a job I *wouldn't* hesitate to share my office with someone who had been mentally ill.

C. *Discussion of the Scales*

Our respondents seem to be combining a spatial closeness with an interaction type of closeness in their responses. More are willing to work for someone who had been mentally ill than are willing to live with him as a neighbor. The difference between an occupational and distant relationship and a personal and friendly relationship is probably the important factor here, and causes social distance from an employer to be perceived as greater than from a neighbor. Similarly, relationship with a fellow office worker is seen as closer than the relationship to those in the next house but less close than to those in the next apartment. It is interesting that although the item, "If I owned an empty lot beside my house I would be willing to sell it to a former mental patient" implies a more permanent tenure of neighborliness than "If I were resident owner of an apartment house I would hesitate to rent living quarters to a former mental hospital patient," the former is easier to respond to positively, probably because the spatial factor allows the respondent to structure one neighborly relationship more distantly than the other.

Association in a club or society is considered a more distant social tie than that of neighborhood or occupational context. Although the working situation, with its "universalistic-performance"[60] qualities, is a distant sort of relationship, small groups have some of the "particularistic quality" characteristic of friendship groups. It is possible, in a town with a rural tradition and composed largely of farmers, many of whom are elderly and retired, that this is even more the case and that the occupational relationships are still thought of in the semikinship terms, as when the "hired man" or the "hired girl" lives with the family. Conversely, the town is highly overorganized and we suspect that the "club or society" is looked upon with ambivalence, being an onerous obligation to some, and an unknown but prestigeful nexus of relationships to others. In such a town we would suppose that membership in an occupational grouping is seen as a closer tie than membership in a voluntary organization.

There is a group of 9 Distance items out of which from 6 to 8 have always formed a scale with our populations. Five of these Distance items scaled in the survey and the resurvey in both Blackfoot and Deerville with reproducibilities of over 90 per cent. These 5 items, which follow below, we call the "Core Distance Scale." They are used for before–after comparisons between the two communities. Similarly, the 4 Responsibility items below, which scaled in both communities the first time, are called the "Core Responsibility Scale" and are used for before–after comparisons.

CORE DISTANCE SCALE

1. We should strongly discourage our children from marrying anyone who has been mentally ill.

2. I can imagine myself falling in love with a person who had been mentally ill.

3. I would be willing to room with a former mental hospital patient.

4. If I owned an empty lot beside my house I would be willing to sell it to a former mental hospital patient.

5. I would be willing to sponsor a person who had been mentally ill for membership in my favorite club or society.

CORE RESPONSIBILITY SCALE

1. Those who live in communities from which mentally sick people come ought to be considered partially responsible for their breakdown.

2. Those who live in communities from which mentally sick people come should be considered to need mental health guidance.

3. The family and friends of a mentally sick person ought to be considered to need mental health guidance.

4. I would feel partially responsible if a member of my family had a serious mental breakdown.

D. *Speculation on "Lost" Items*

The following Responsibility items were excluded in all scaling operations because their high error shows that they do not belong on a single dimension.

1. I can imagine myself becoming mentally ill (31.7 per cent positive).

2. I would be willing to take training which would make me eligible to sponsor a mental hospital patient when he was discharged (40.1 per cent positive).

3. I would feel no personal responsibility if a member of my favorite club or society became mentally ill (51.7 per cent positive).

4. In spite of our best efforts there is very little which we can do to prevent mental illness (67.6 per cent positive).

5. Our community should not be expected to take the responsibility of providing suitable jobs for its former mental hospital patients (68.9 per cent positive).

6. It would be wise to discourage former mental hospital patients from entering our community since they are likely to become an expense (80.7 per cent positive).

7. Only professionally trained people such as doctors, or ministers, should feel responsibility for other people's problems of mental health and mental illness (81.1 per cent positive).

It is interesting that the only item with the term "personal responsibility" failed to scale. Two-thirds of the population said they would take this kind of responsibility for a fellow club member, but apparently this attitude is not in the same dimension as the other items which only use the bare word "responsibility." We are inclined to think that this fortifies our interpretation that the scale measures a dimension of general "responsibleness" rather than a specific kind of responsibility such as this item suggests.

That even 20 per cent of our respondents think that total exclusion of former mental hospital patients from the community is desirable is grimly interesting, as is the fact that about 20 per cent (not necessarily the same 20 per cent) think only professionally trained people should feel any responsibility for others' problems and illnesses. Again, only

31.7 per cent of respondents can imagine themselves as mentally ill, suggesting that the other 68.3 per cent completely dissociate themselves from this form of deviation.

The following Distance items were lost because too high an error score rendered them unscaleable. They are again listed in order of frequency of success.

1. I would marry a member of a family in which there is mental illness (41.5 per cent positive).

2. I would be willing to trust someone who had been mentally ill with financial matters (49.8 per cent positive).

3. I would never trust anyone who had been mentally ill with my children (54.6 per cent positive).

4. I would not lend money to a person who had been mentally ill (71.1 per cent positive).

Evidently the whole question of financial transaction is inappropriate in this scale. Here the universalistic-performance[60] nature of the market relationship seems dominant; decisions about financial matters are not made on the basis of the past personal misfortunes of the other party to the transaction.

Discarded items 1 and 3 above appear logically related to Scale items, "We should strongly discourage our children from marrying anyone who has been mentally ill" and "I can imagine myself falling in love with someone who had been mentally ill" but apparently have meaning to the respondents which remove them from the continuum. One might speculate that attitudes toward the "in-law" problem have contaminated the "marrying into a family" item and that response to the "looking after the children" item varies with whether or not the respondent has children. Some evidence for this resides in the fact that our series of childless student nurses made so many successful responses to this item that it was discarded, suggesting that attitudes toward children are dominant here rather than attitudes toward mental illness. Further work should clarify the latent meanings of the responses to all of these items. Fortunately, for our purpose the scales are expected to operate as *general* indices of distance and responsibility, and our focus is not on the precise meanings of individual terms, but rather on changes in the scores on groups of items in whose general meaning we are interested.

E. *Speculation Regarding Failure of Correlation between Scales*

As we have said in the text, there is no logical reason for expecting a relationship between our scales, but rather a need to explain our expectation of relationship. However, before resorting to this task it is as well to entertain the idea that either an artifact or a methodological error has masked a genuine relationship.

There have been two attempts to demonstrate that there are two kinds of respondents whose responses cancel each other out and thus leave a spurious unrelatedness. One attempt postulates different personality types among respondents and the other postulates that people who responded to "responsibility for cause" differed from those who responded "responsibility for care." It is conceivable that this could happen, but it is hard to imagine that the scale error would stay within acceptable limits (10 per cent) if this were the case, because it would really imply two interleaved scales which gave the appearance of one solid scale. On the whole we confess that we are dissatisfied with these explanations. We feel that this unrelatedness may well be a methodological matter, but we do not feel that the postulate of two insulated nexuses of attitudes, which we have spelled out in the text, is without merit. It suffers scientifically from being *post hoc* and would therefore need empirical demonstration, but we believe that the effort to make such an empirical demonstration would be well worth while.

The Interview

A. *The Form*

The design of our experiment included the use of the following lengthy "open-ended" interview which we borrowed from Dr. Shirley A. Star of the National Opinion Research Center, Chicago, Illinois. She had developed this instrument for a national survey of opinion regarding mental illness. With it we hoped to discover from a random sample of our population what sorts of facts and theories lay behind their responses to the questionnaires about attitudes toward mental illness which we had administered upon first entering the community. Very few of the responses to this questionnaire are analyzed in this volume, but a full account will be available in Dr. Star's forthcoming book.

1. A. What would you say is the most serious disease today? (I mean, what illness would be the worst one for a person to have?)
   B. Why is [name of illness] the most serious one?
2. When was the last time you were sick enough to see a doctor?
3. What was the matter? What illness did you have?
4. Of course, everybody hears a good deal about physical illness and disease, but now, what about the ones we call *mental* or nervous illness? When you hear some one say that a person is "mentally ill," what does that mean to you? (PROBES: How would you describe a person who is mentally ill? What do you think a mentally ill person is like? What does a person like this do that tells you he is mentally ill? How does a person like this act?)
5. Would you say that everyone who has a mental illness is out of

his mind? (A) [If "NOT INSANE" or "DEPENDS"] What is the matter with the ones who aren't insane then?

6. A. As far as you know, what is a nervous breakdown? (PROBES: How would you describe it? What is it like? What happens to a person who has one? How does he act?)

   B. Would you say that a nervous breakdown is a mental illness or not? (I) [If "IS," "IS NOT," or "DEPENDS" to B] What are your reasons for saying so?

7. Now I'd like to describe a certain kind of person and ask you a few questions about him. I'm thinking of a man . . . let's call him Frank Jones . . . who is very suspicious; he doesn't trust anybody, and he's sure that everybody is against him. Sometimes he thinks that people he sees on the street are talking about him or following him around. A couple of times, now, he has beaten up men who didn't even know him, because he thought that they were plotting against him. The other night, he began to curse his wife terribly; then he hit her and threatened to kill her, because, he said, she was working against him, too, just like everyone else.

   Would you say that there is anything wrong with this man, or not?

   [If "SOMETHING WRONG" or "DON'T KNOW," ask A and B.
   If "NOTHING WRONG," ask A.]

   A. What do you think makes him act this way? (PROBES: What's causing him to act like this? What happened to him to make him like this?)

   [ASK B OF EVERYONE EXCEPT "NOTHING WRONG" TO QUESTION 7.]

   B. Would you say this man . . . Frank Jones . . . has some kind of mental illness or not?

      (1) Why do you say that he has (does not have) a mental illness?

      (2) Would you say that the mental illness he has is a serious one or not? (a) [If "SERIOUS," "NOT SERIOUS," or "DEPENDS"] Why do you say it is (is not) serious?

8. Now here's a young woman in her twenties, let's call her Betty Smith. . . . She has never had a job, and she doesn't seem to want to go out and look for one. She is a very quiet girl, she doesn't talk much to anyone . . . she doesn't even talk much to her own family, and she acts like she is afraid of people, especially young men her own age. She won't go out with anyone, and whenever someone comes to visit her family, she stays in her own room until

they leave. She just stays by herself and daydreams all the time, and shows no interest in anything or anybody.

Would you say that there is anything wrong with this young woman or not? SPONTANEOUS COMMENT:

[If "SOMETHING WRONG," or "DON'T KNOW" to 8, ask A and B. If "NOTHING WRONG," ask A.]

A. What do you think makes her act this way? (PROBES: What's causing her to act like this? What happened to make her like this?)

B. Would you say this young woman—Betty Smith—has some kind of mental illness or not?

[If "HAS" or "DEPENDS," ask (1) and (2). If "HAS NOT," ask (1).]

  (1) Why do you say that she has (does not have) a mental illness?

  (2) Would you say that the mental illness she has is a serious one or not?

    (a) [If "SERIOUS," "NOT SERIOUS," or "DEPENDS"] Why do you say it is so?

9. Here's another kind of man; we can call him George Brown. He has a good job and is doing pretty well at it. Most of the time he gets along all right with people, but he is always very touchy and he always loses his temper quickly, if things aren't going his way, or if people find fault with him. He worries a lot about little things, and he seems to be moody and unhappy all the time. Everything is going along all right for him, but he can't sleep nights, brooding about the past, and worrying about things that *might* go wrong.

Would you say that there is anything wrong with this man or not?

[If "SOMETHING WRONG," or "DON'T KNOW," ask A and B. If "NOTHING WRONG," ask A.]

A. What do you think makes him act this way? (PROBE: What's causing him to act so?)

[ASK B OF EVERYONE EXCEPT "NOTHING WRONG" TO QUESTION 9.]

B. Would you say this man—George Brown—has some kind of mental illness or not?

  (1) Why do you say that he has (does not have) a mental illness?

(2) Would you say that the mental illness he has is serious or not?

    (*a*) [If "SERIOUS," "NOT SERIOUS," or "DEPENDS"] Why do you say so?

10. How about Bill Williams? He never seems to be able to hold a job very long, because he drinks so much. Whenever he has money in his pocket, he goes on a spree; he stays out till all hours drinking, and never seems to care what happens to his wife and children. Sometimes, he feels very bad about the way he treats his family; he begs his wife to forgive him and promises to stop drinking, but he always goes off again.

Would you say that there is anything wrong with this man or not?

A. What do you think makes him act this way? (PROBE: What's causing him to act so?)

B. Would you say this man—Bill Williams—has some kind of mental illness or not?

[If "HAS" or "DEPENDS," ask (1) and (2).

If "HAS NOT," ask (1).]

    (1) Why do you say that he has (does not have) a mental illness?

    (2) Would you say that the mental illness he has is serious, or not?

        (*a*) [If "SERIOUS," "NOT SERIOUS," or "DEPENDS"] Why do you say it is so?

11. Here's a different sort of girl—let's call her Mary White. She seems happy and cheerful, she's pretty, has a good enough job, and is engaged to marry a nice young man. She has loads of friends: everybody likes her, and she's always busy and active. However, she just can't leave the house without going back to see whether she left the gas stove lit or not. And she always goes back again just to make sure she locked the door. And one other thing about her; she's afraid to ride up and down in elevators; she just won't go any place where she'd have to ride in an elevator to get there.

[If "SOMETHING WRONG" or "DON'T KNOW," ask A and B.

If "NOTHING WRONG," ask A.]

A. What do you think makes her act this way? (PROBE: What's causing her to act so?)

[ASK B OF EVERYONE EXCEPT "NOTHING WRONG" TO QUESTION 11.]

B. Would you say that this young woman—Mary White—has some kind of mental illness or not?

[If "HAS" or "DEPENDS," ask (1) and (2).

If "HAS NOT," ask (1).]

(1) Why do you say that she has (does not have) a mental illness?

(2) Would you say that the mental illness she has is a serious one or not?

(a) [If "SERIOUS," "NOT SERIOUS," or "DEPENDS"] Why do you say it is so?

12. Now, the last person I'd like to describe is a twelve-year-old boy —Bobby Grey. He's bright enough and in good health, and he comes from a comfortable home. But his father and mother have found out that he's been telling lies for a long time now. He's been stealing things from stores, and taking money from his mother's purse, and he has been playing truant, staying away from school whenever he can. His parents are very upset about the way he acts, but he pays no attention to them.

Would you say that there is anything wrong with this boy or not?

[If "SOMETHING WRONG" or "DON'T KNOW" to 12, ask A. and B. If "NOTHING WRONG," ask A.]

A. What do you think makes him act this way? (PROBES: What's causing him to act like this? What happened to make him like this?)

B. Would you say this boy—Bobby Grey—has some kind of mental illness or not?

[If "HAS" or "DEPENDS," ask (1) and (2).

If "HAS NOT," ask (1).]

(1) Why do you say that he has (does not have) a mental illness?

(2) Would you say that the mental illness he has is a serious one or not?

(a) [If "SERIOUS," "NOT SERIOUS," or "DEPENDS"] Why do you say it is so?

13. Well, we've been talking about different kinds of people and what makes them act the way they do. . . . Now let's talk about people who go out of their minds, go insane. What causes people to go out of their minds? (What else could cause people to go insane?)

14. Now, how about people who aren't out of their minds, but do have emotional problems or nervous conditions. . . . Would you

say that these less severe nervous conditions have the same causes as insanity or not?

A. (If "DIFFERENT" or "SOME SAME, SOME DIFFERENT") What would you say causes people to get into these less severe nervous conditions? (Can you think of anything else which would cause nervous conditions in people?)

15. [Hand respondent card] Now here is a list of different things that could happen to people. . . .

A. Is there anything on this list which would be enough, by itself, to cause people to have an emotional or nervous sickness, without losing their minds? Which ones? (Any others?)

(1) Too much brain work
(2) Drinking too much
(3) Not enough will-power, lack of self-control
(4) Masturbation (playing with oneself, self-abuse)
(5) Sex habits
(6) Money troubles
(7) Trouble getting along with one's husband or wife
(8) Trouble getting on the job
(9) A run-down physical condition
(10) Growing old
(11) Not being loved as a child
(12) Poor heredity, family inheritance (a family history of this kind of sickness)

      All of them
      None of them
      Combination of them
      Don't know

B. Is there anything on this list which would be enough, by itself, to cause people to lose their minds? Which ones? (Any others?)

[RECORD RESPONSES ABOVE.]

C. [If "SEX HABITS" or "ALL OF THEM" to A or B] You just said that sex habits might cause people to develop nervous conditions or lose their minds. What did you have in mind? (Were you thinking of anything else? What?)

16. Now, talking about people who have these nervous conditions, without being out of their minds: Do you think people who have these less severe nervous conditions can get over them or not?

A. [If "CAN" or "SOME CAN"] Can they get over these nervous

conditions *by themselves* or do they *need help* to get over them?
[If "BY THEMSELVES," ask (1).
If "NEED HELP," ask (2) and (3).
If "BOTH" or "DEPENDS," ask (1), (2), and (3).]

(1) What can they do by themselves to get better? (Anything else?)

(2) Who could help them with their problems? (Anyone else?)

[If "DOCTOR," PROBE: Any special kind of doctor?]

(3) What do you think these people could do that would help?

17. Is there anything that can be done to keep a person from getting these nervous conditions?
[If "YES," ask A.
If "NO," ask B.
If "DEPENDS," ask A. and B.]
A. What can be done? (Anything else?) [If "DOCTOR," PROBE: Any special kind of doctor?]
B. Why not? (Why can't anything be done?)

18. A. What do you suppose you would do if you were worried about someone in your family (or someone close to you) who was not acting like himself? (I mean, suppose someone in your family started acting like some of the people we have been talking about, what would you do about it?) [If "DOCTOR," PROBE: Any special kind of doctor?]
B. [If any answer other than "SEEK PSYCHIATRIC ADVICE"] Suppose that didn't work. . . . What would you do next? (If "DOCTOR," PROBE: Any special kind of doctor?)

19. Now let's take a person who loses his mind. . . . Once this person goes out of his mind, is there anything that can be done to help him get better again?
[If "YES," ask A.
If "NO," ask B.
If "DEPENDS," ask A. and B.]
A. What can be done for him? (Anything else?) [If "DOCTOR," PROBE: Any special kind of doctor?]
B. Why not? (Why can't anything be done?)

20. Do you think a person who goes out of his mind should be placed in a mental hospital (asylum) or not?

(1) [If "SHOULD," "SHOULD NOT," or "DEPENDS"] Why

do you think he should (should not) be placed in a mental hospital?

21. Do you think anything can be done beforehand to keep a person from losing his mind?
[If "YES," ask A.
If "NO," ask B.
If "DEPENDS," ask A. and B.]
A. What could be done? (Anything else?) [If "DOCTOR," PROBE: Any special kind of doctor?]
B. Why not? (Why couldn't anything be done?)

22. Do you think that *most* of the people who lose their minds stay that way or do *most* of them get well again?
A. [If "MOST STAY THAT WAY" or "ABOUT HALF AND HALF"] Why is it that so many of them don't get well?

23. In general, would you say that a person who goes out of his mind can get *completely* well again, or would he always show some signs of having been mentally ill once?

24. Do you think *most* insane people are dangerous to be around, or not?
A. [If "ARE"] What makes it dangerous to be around them?

25. Do you think it might do people harm in *any* (*other*) way to be around someone who is insane?
A. [If "YES" or "DEPENDS"] How might it be harmful?

26. If you found out that someone you knew who seemed all right now had been in a mental hospital (asylum) once, do you think you'd *feel* any different about being around this person?
[If "WOULD FEEL DIFFERENT," ask A.
If "NO DIFFERENT" or "DON'T KNOW," ask B.
If "DEPENDS," ask A. and B.]
A. How do you think you'd feel about being around him (her)?
B. Do you think you would *treat* a person who had once been in a mental hospital any differently than you treat other people? (How would you treat him (her)?)

27. Do you think that most people would feel the same way that you do about being around a person who had once been in a mental hospital (asylum) or not?
A. [If "DIFFERENT"] How do you think most people would feel about being around this person?

28. Did you ever know anyone who was in a hospital (asylum) because of a mental illness?

A. [If "YES"] Was this a relative, a close friend, or just someone you didn't know very well?

29. Of course, you know that sometimes people who have mental illnesses or nervous problems go to *psychiatrists* (doctors who specialize in treating mental illness and nervous conditions) for help. . . . As you see it, how serious a problem should a person have before he goes to see a psychiatrist? (Why?)

30. As far as you know, how does a psychiatrist go about helping the people who come to him? [If "TALK," PROBE: After he finds this out, what does he do?]

31. Have you ever known anyone (other than persons mentioned in Question 28) who was seeing a psychiatrist, without being in a mental hospital (asylum) or going to a guidance or mental hygiene clinic?
[If "YES," ask A. and B.]
A. Was this a relative, a close friend, or just someone you didn't know very well?
    Respondent . . .
    Immediate family . . .
    Other relatives . . .
    Close friends . . .
    Acquaintances . . .
    Other (specify) . . .
    Won't say . . .
B. Do you think this person was really helped (is really being helped) by this treatment?
    (1) [If "NO" to B.] Why isn't the treatment helping (didn't the treatment help)?

32. Do you know any (other) people who you think would be helped if they'd see a psychiatrist?
A. [If "YES"] Why do you suppose they don't see one? (Are there any other reasons why they wouldn't see a psychiatrist?)

33. Well, you know, it's been said that a lot of us would be helped if we'd see a psychiatrist about some of our problems. . . . Do you think *you* would want to see a psychiatrist?
[If "YES," ask A.
If "NO," ask B.]
A. What would you want to see a psychiatrist about?
B. Why not? (Any other reasons?)

34. Well, we've been talking about all these problems of mental health and mental illness. Now I'd like to ask you where you've gotten

most of your information about these things. . . . Have you ever:
(*a*) Read anything in the *newspapers* about mental health problems?
(*b*) Read any *magazine articles* about mental health problems?
(*c*) Read any *books* about mental health problems?
(*d*) Seen any *movies* about mental health problems?
(*e*) Heard any *radio programs* about mental health problems?
(*f*) Heard any *lectures or talks* about mental health problems?
(*g*) Talked with *your doctor* about mental health problems?
(*h*) Talked with your *family and friends* about mental health problems?
(*i*) Seen or heard *anything else* about mental health problems? [SPECIFY SOURCE.]

35. You know, some experts say that one out of every ten people in Canada will have some kind of mental illness or nervous condition in the course of their lives. And right now, over half the hospital beds in the country are occupied by people who are mentally ill. . . .

    What do you think can be done about this problem—the large amount of mental illness in this country?

B. *The Sample*

We wanted 100 interviews before the educational program and 100 afterward. From a list of all the adults (18 years and over) in the community which had been compiled by the Town Clerk a month previously, we chose a systematic sample.* These people were all approached for interviews, but during the process we discovered that many who were technically citizens of Blackfoot did not live there at all. Of the 300 people selected from the list, we interviewed 178: 100 before the program and 78 afterward. (All names were selected before the experiment to insure that no newcomers, who had not been exposed to the program, would be included in the second group.) Ninety people in the sample were absent from the town either temporarily or for an extended period, and 32 refused to be interviewed. Most of these refusals were in the second interview.

There is a certain important source of bias in this sample of interviews: some people were adamant in their refusal to be interviewed on

---

* We are grateful to the Dominion Bureau of Statistics, Ottawa, for advice and guidance regarding the selection of samples in Blackfoot and Deerville.

the subject, and one can only assume that their refusal is a reflection in some measure of their thinking about mental illness and that this thinking differs in relevant ways from the thinking of those willing to be interviewed. Extreme persuasion was not used because the type of interviewing we were doing, in which the respondent is encouraged to unfold his thinking on the subject, requires willingness and cooperation from the respondent. It is quite possible for a recalcitrant subject to conceal his opinions by answering, "I don't know" to many of the questions about which he, in fact, has an opinion.

We have reason to suspect that some important information was lost because a few people who had recently had family members committed to a mental hospital refused the interview. Unfortunately we cannot correct for this loss.

The interviews were conducted by a team of 6 social workers and clinical psychologists whom we trained to conduct neutral research interviews. They were expected to probe each question asked until the rock-bottom of the respondent's thinking about mental illness had been reached. There may be less detail in our interviews than in those conducted by professional public opinion interviewers because our interviewers were by their professions accustomed to attempting to lower the anxiety of their respondents rather than to extracting the maximum information from them. All probes were neutral, that is, were not leading questions. All responses were recorded verbatim.

Reports collected from the interviewers as they left the field indicated a good reception. The citizens were polite and cooperative; if an interview was obtained at all it was very pleasant. All interviewers expressed interest in returning to the field for the second interview in the spring, finding it an enjoyable interlude from clinical work. All interviews were checked to insure that the records of the answers were complete and legible.